Christianity and Social Engagement in China

How does Christianity continue to experience growth in an increasingly authoritarian political system that enforces strict regulations on religion? How are ordinary Christians affected by social and political changes in the country, and how do they make their influence felt in wider society?

Taking Chinese Christians' experience as a case study, Lim and Sng examine the possibilities and limitations of Christian engagement in society under an authoritarian regime. They look especially at efforts by religious individuals and groups who are seeking to address social issues by engaging in unobtrusive and non-antagonistic activities that interact with controlling state institutions. Their emphasis is on everyday lived religion, analysing how Christians express their faith in their everyday activity and not only in spaces demarcated as falling within the religious domain.

This book is a valuable reference for scholars and students looking to understand religion in relation to politics, culture and everyday life in rapidly modernising East Asian societies and particularly in China.

Francis K.G. Lim is Associate Professor in the Social Sciences at Nanyang Technological University, Singapore.

Bee Bee Sng is an Adjunct Lecturer in Research Methodology and Academic Writing Skills in several universities in Singapore and supervises trainee teachers at the National Institute of Education, Singapore.

Routledge Religion in Contemporary Asia Series
Series Editor: Bryan S. Turner, Professor at the City University of New York and Director of the Centre for Religion and Society at the University of Western Sydney

3 **Thailand's International Meditation Centers**
Tourism and the Global Commodification of Religious Practices
Brooke Schedneck

4 **Digital Culture and Religion in Asia**
Sam Han and Kamaludeen Mohamed Nasir

5 **Being Catholic in the Contemporary Philippines**
Jayeel Serrano Cornelio

6 **Catholics and Everyday Life in Macau**
Changing Meanings of Religiosity, Morality and Civility
Chen Hon Fai

7 **Sufi Political Thought**
Milad Milani

8 **Modernist Reformers in Islam, Hinduism and Confucianism, 1865–1935**
Peripheral Geoculture in the Modern World-System
Christian Lekon

9 **Religion and Religious Practices in Rural China**
Mu Peng

10 **Christianity and Social Engagement in China**
Francis K.G. Lim and Bee Bee Sng

11 **Ethnicity and Religion in Southwest China**
He Ming and David C. Lewis

Christianity and Social Engagement in China

Francis K.G. Lim and Bee Bee Sng

Routledge
Taylor & Francis Group
LONDON AND NEW YORK

First published 2021
by Routledge
2 Park Square, Milton Park, Abingdon, Oxon OX14 4RN

and by Routledge
52 Vanderbilt Avenue, New York, NY 10017

Routledge is an imprint of the Taylor & Francis Group, an informa business

British Library Cataloguing-in-Publication Data
A catalogue record for this book is available from the British Library

Library of Congress Cataloging-in-Publication Data
Names: Lim, Francis K. H., 1949– author. | Sng, Bee Bee, author.
Title: Christianity and social engagement in China /
Francis Lim, Bee Bee Sng.
Description: Abingdon, Oxon; New York: Routledge, 2021. |
Series: Religion in contemporary Asia |
Includes bibliographical references and index. |
Identifiers: LCCN 2020031808 (print) |
LCCN 2020031809 (ebook) | ISBN 9780367439224 (hbk) |
ISBN 9781003006503 (ebk)
Subjects: LCSH: China—Church history. | Church and state—
China—History. | Christianity and politics—China—History. |
Christians—Political activity—China.
Classification: LCC BR1285 .L4645 2021 (print) |
LCC BR1285 (ebook) | DDC 306.6/30951—dc23
LC record available at https://lccn.loc.gov/2020031808
LC ebook record available at https://lccn.loc.gov/2020031809

ISBN: 978-0-367-43922-4 (hbk)
ISBN: 978-1-003-00650-3 (ebk)

Typeset in Galliard
by codeMantra

Contents

Figures

Acknowledgements

In the course of our research for this book, we have received generous support from a number of institutions. We are also grateful to many individuals for their encouragement, advice, and camaraderie that have sustained our effort in the past few years.

From the beginning, our research received strong support from Alan Chan, former Dean of the College of Humanities, Arts and Social Sciences; and Liu Hong, former Chair, School of Social Sciences. We would also like to acknowledge the financial assistance provided by the NTU New Silk Road Grant and the Ministry of Education AcRF Tier 1 Grant for our study. We thank Simon Bates, editor at Routledge, for having patiently guided us in the publication process.

We owe a huge debt to all the people who have so kindly given us their time in response to our multiple queries and requests for interviews. Tobias Brandner at the Chinese University of Hong Kong kindly introduced us to some important interviewees in Hong Kong. We thank the Christian communities in our fieldwork sites who have warmly welcomed us into their midst to interview them about their beliefs and activities. Many of our respondents were sincere and candid in sharing with us their opinions on the development of Christianity in an increasingly challenging political context in China. Without them, our research would not have been possible. Unfortunately, we are unable to name these individuals due to the need for strict anonymity.

This study can be seen as an integral part of the continual research on religion in a restrictive environment. It stands on the shoulders of giants. We are very fortunate to have found inspiration in the work and support of fellow scholars as we strove to find our way forward. First and foremost, Shirley Sun offered critical feedback and valuable suggestions to sharpen some arguments in the book. We have also found inspiration from the following scholars whose work on religion in China have influenced our own work: Robert Weller, Richard Madsen, Yang Fenggang, Kenneth Dean, Cao Nanlai, Susan McCarthy, Khun Eng Kuah-Pearce, Carsten Vala, Wu Keping, Chan Shun-hing, André Laliberté, Adam Chau, David Palmer, and Ji Zhe.

We are immensely thankful for the opportunities to present parts of our research at a number of academic workshops and conferences. First, this research was presented at the Ethics of Religious Giving Conference at the Asia Research

Institute, where Michael Feener, Thomas Borchert and Wu Keping provided critical comments to improve the discussion of holistic development. We are grateful to Lin Wei-ping at the National Taiwan University for the invitation to present a paper in the Religion in City Space and Cyberspace Workshop. In addition, Cao Nanlai and Wei Dedong at Renmin University kindly invited one of us to participate in the 16th China Social Scientific Study of Religion. In this event, we received insightful feedback from Robert Weller, Giuseppe Giordan, and Kang Jie. Finally, we would like to express our appreciation to Sakurai Yoshihide, Hokkaido University, for the opportunity to participate in the International Symposium on Globalization and Religious Cultures in East Asia at the Kokugakuin University. Some versions of the work have also benefitted from discussions at the International Sociological Association conference in Vienna, the Australian Sociology Association conference in Perth, and the AAS-in-Asia conference in Singapore.

Last but not least, we are deeply grateful to our respective families for their support and understanding during our research.

1 Gifts from above

Christianity and social engagement in China

This particular Qiang ethnic community lived in the innermost mountainous area in Sichuan. Surrounded by pristine mountains, the area they lived was inaccessible by road to outsiders. The Qiang were proud of their heritage, and claimed that one of their ancestors was an emperor of China. Donned in brightly coloured costumes, the women generally wore dresses in bright crimson embroidered flowers and carried purses of similar brightly embroidered flowers. They lived in houses with flat square roofs which had small piles of white stones at each corner of the square roof. The small piles of stones were religious in meaning and symbolised the horns of goats which they worshipped. In their town stood a tall tower in which was also a significant site of their religious worship. Much of their livelihood was agricultural. They grew crops and reared goats. Surrounded by the tall mountains, much of their cultural tradition seemed shielded from outside influences. It was hard to imagine that anything in the world would disrupt the life that the Qiang lived in this ethnic autonomous region by the Mianyang river. However, in this afternoon, a calamitous event would change their life forever.

The children were soundly asleep in the warm afternoon. Zhang Mo (pseudonym), the head prefect of the school, was doing his usual round of walking down the passageway of the classrooms to ensure that the children were safe. Zhang Mo was in the graduating senior high class. He had contemplated about his future and desired to study medicine in a university in the city. He was anxious that his chances would be slim, knowing the stiff competition for the limited places for medicine for a city university. His entry level to the course would be determined by both his performance in the state examinations and ranking of his school. Being an ethnic minority school, it was extremely hard for the school to compete in ranking with schools in the cities which enjoyed more resources such as better teaching materials, equipment, better trained teachers, and even foreign teachers who taught English language to boost the students' English proficiency. English was a big factor that influenced the ranking of the schools, as China was in the midst of improving its standard of English in order to be recognised globally.

As Zhang Mo reached the second level of the school, he felt a tremor. Suddenly, he realised it could be an earthquake since the Ngawa Tibetan and Qiang Autonomous Prefecture was located on major fault lines.

Zhang Mo quickly woke all the children in the classrooms. ***Kuai, kuai tao! dizhen jiu yao fasheng le!*** 'Quickly, escape quickly! An earthquake is going to happen!' The children dashed out of their classrooms, out of the school building into the open square. As the children ran with all their might, the tremor grew stronger. The roof of the ceiling came clashing down and eventually, the second floor buckled and clashed to the ground.

This was the devastating earthquake that happened in Sichuan in 2008. At that time, one of us had been involved in voluntary work in the GMV (pseudonym), a foreign Christian NGO. She received a telephone call from the GMV office to help recruit doctors, nurses, physiotherapists, and counsellors to go to the earthquake-affected area in Sichuan for trauma therapy work. In the weeks that ensued, she visited churches, gave presentations on the carnage of the earthquake, and recruited several medical personnel for the earthquake relief work. The trauma doctors performed orthopaedic surgeries on the victims; the physiotherapists conducted rehabilitation to help the victims with the use of their arms and legs again, and the counsellors conducted therapy on post-traumatic stress disorder. Exactly one year from the time of the earthquake, in June 2009, one of us went to the school described above to conduct an intensive summer English course for the children.

Recently, while commemorating the sixtieth anniversary of the China Three-Self Patriotic Movement, the leader of the China Christian Council, Chan Baoping, highlights the imperative to "Sinicise" Christianity and prevent "foreign forces" from influencing the religion in China. He also emphasises that Chinese Christianity, instead of seeking to transform society, should now take serving society as its main task. A Sinicised Christianity should also support the nation building agenda of the ruling Chinese Communist Party (CCP). Chan's underlying message implies this: if Christians aimed to transform society, they might mobilise and challenge the status quo, including existing political structures and the authority of the Communist Party over the Church. This book addresses two important questions regarding Christianity in China: First, how does Christianity continue to experience growth in an ever-increasingly authoritarian political system that enforces strict regulations on religion? Second, how are ordinary Christians affected by social and political changes in the country, and how do they make the influence of their faith felt in the wider society? By focusing on the Chinese Christians' experiences as a case study, this book will contribute to the broader scholarship on religious social engagement, especially in authoritarian socialist regimes like China that practise some forms of atheist secularism.

An outline of Christianity and social change[1]

In this book, we explore the community development work of the GMV and Chinese Christians' engagement with social media. We also investigate their views on work and the workplace from a Christian perspective. These themes elucidate the questions of how Chinese Christians view their society and their role in transforming their society through what they view as positive attitudes and behaviour, as well as charitable acts, in society. These themes are embodied in the overarching concept of Christianity and social change. That Christians in China and elsewhere may wish to transform society is nothing new. Throughout the history of Christianity, we can discern clear theological and practical emphases on the role of the church in social change. The Church has always played an active role "in the life of humankind, in making of nationhood, building of culture, structuring of society with its functions and institutions and in shaping the form and quality of political systems" (Pillay 2017: 1). The role that Christianity plays in social change can be initially viewed from a close examination of Jesus' teachings. Jesus' teachings are located within a socio-economic and political context. Hence, socio-economic and political factors have a large influence on his teachings. Jesus, in his teachings in the Bible, emphasised the importance for his followers to care for the poor and marginalised. He defended the poor and marginalised before the Pharisees and Sadducees, and, in turn, criticised the self-indulgence and greed of the latter (Matthew 23: 25–33). The Pharisees and Sadducees were known for their exploitation and oppression of the poor and marginalised. In Jesus' teachings, it was noticeably clear that he was on the side of the weak and poor in society. He taught that the Kingdom of God belongs to these marginalised in society (Luke 6: 20–26), and the harlots and tax-collectors would gain entry to the Kingdom of God before those who were religious and respected in society (Matthew 21: 31–32). Thus, from the early days of the founding of Christianity, the mission of the church has always been to transform the individual and community. Therefore, these teachings form the source of motivation of Christians' charitable acts in society and their concept of social change, which differ significantly from the general thinking about social change.

The early Christians did not intentionally restructure society by confronting socio-economic justice. Rather, they helped the poor and marginalised out of love and compassion as taught in scriptures. In this sense, efforts to address and eradicate social inequality was not an extra function of the church, which is separate from its main function, but is very much the central focus of the church's role in society. However, even though the church drew up guidelines for helping the poor, often it allowed the rich to remain comfortable. In this, Pillay (2017) argues, the early church only tackled the consequences of poverty and did not deal with the structural and institutional roots of poverty. Instead, it allowed the poor to continue to be dependent on the rich. In comparison, the overarching goal of the GMV, a faith-based organisation (FBO) that we will be discussing later, is to eradicate poverty in the communities it works in by empowering the poor with skills that they need to mobilise themselves socially and economically up the social ladder. GMV holds the position that the Chinese rural poor should not be perpetually dependent on them, but should be trained in skills so that they can be self-sufficient and contribute ultimately to the development of their own communities.

There are three shifts that need to happen in the church for its aim to transform the individual and community to be accomplished. First, the church needs to look outwards, beyond its four walls, and not focus only on its internal affairs.

Second, the church needs to move from a focus on programme to an emphasis on people development. Third, it needs to move from being focused on the church to being kingdom focused, namely, to have a global perspective of the influence of Christianity (Pillay 2017). Arguably, these three shifts of the church can be discerned in some of the most significant Christian theological and social movements (both Protestant and Catholic) which are sweeping the globe in recent decades (Jenkins 2011). In terms of Christianity's cultural impact and social engagement, one of the most notable phenomena in Asian Christianity in recent years is the rise of Pentecostalism and Charismatic movements that mirrors the development of global Christianity. In *Pentecostalism: The World Their Parish*, David Martin (2002) has charted the tremendous growth of Pentecostalism around the world and noted how this singular event has exerted powerful impacts on areas such as politics, sociocultural change, economic development, and geopolitical alliances. Meanwhile, the more traditional Christian denominations have also evolved in response to the rise of Pentecostalism and charismatic movements. These movements incorporate new ways of worship and initiate programmes for institutional reforms. In China and the rest of Asia, increasing numbers of Pentecostals and charismatics are advocating a pragmatic and contextual gospel that motivate them to participate actively in social movements that push for cultural change and preservation; political reforms; social equality; healing and spirituality; the pursuit of success and prosperity, etc. (Anderson 2014: 169). In short, Christianity has historically been a powerful force for social change in Asia (Bautista and Lim 2009).

Christian social engagement in China: an historical review

Studies on the arrival of Christianity in China have demonstrated how the religion has been profoundly impactful on Chinese society and culture (Lin 1993; Charbonnier 2007; Bays 2012). One of the earliest efforts by Catholic missionaries to change China was to introduce "new knowledge" to the imperial court. The main purpose was to illustrate both the superiority of Western knowledge and its associated religion, namely, Christianity. For the Jesuits who were very active in the Ming and Qing courts, the imperative was to first convert the Emperor and his inner circles of relatives and court officials. The missiological principle was based on the Jesuits' conviction that the conversion of the highest echelon of society's elite would result in the subsequent conversion of the whole society.

In order to understand the history of Christian social engagement in China, it is necessary to discuss the rise of missionary societies in the West.[2] At the end of the 18th century, new missionary societies proliferated in all Protestant countries such as Great Britain, Germany, the Netherlands, Switzerland, the Scandinavian countries, and the United States (Bosch 2007). In 1880s, with the start of the high imperial era, there was a second wave of new societies forming, with the United States taking the lead in terms of the highest number of missionaries being sent overseas. The end of World War II saw another surge of passion and new missionary societies forming. In the period of 40 years, between 1900 and 1939, 147 new missionary societies were formed. In the next 40 years, 1940 to 1949, 83 societies sprung up, followed by 395 new agencies in the period of 1950 to 1979.

A few factors were probably responsible for this wave of enthusiasm. It is undeniable that the spirit of enterprise and initiative sparked the formation and proliferation of the missionary societies. Before this, the formation of "voluntary societies" (Bosch 2007: 328) next to the institutional church was unheard of. The institutional church remained the nexus of control and sending agency of missionaries. At the end of the 17th century, however, a new attitude emerged. The Reformation belief of the right of private interpretation of Scripture led to the thinking that a group of people could unite to promote a common cause. This led to a superfluity of new societies. They promoted a variety of religious and societal concerns such as "antislavery, prison reform, temperance, sabbath observance" (Bosch 2007: 328) and other charitable concerns. Many of these new societies ventured overseas and promoted the cause of foreign missions. Many of the missionaries who travelled abroad were women and these societies were all organised around the principle of volunteerism, totally dependent on the members' time, energy, and money. These societies were based on the social and political egalitarianism of democracy that was rising at that time. There was a central office that received donations from auxiliary associations and sent information to these branches. People of average incomes many thousand miles away contributed both money and prayer support. The Enlightenment's optimistic perspective of the world and humanity led to the people's belief that they could do something about their circumstances and those of others. The believers formed goal-oriented communities and held a firm belief that they were God's co-workers in ushering in the Kingdom of God.

Fifty years after the Independence in the United States, interdenominational mission societies were formed. Among these was the London Missionary Society (LMS) which was founded in 1795. The LMS was founded by the same principle that William Carey proposed in 1792 which is mainly business-like, instrumental, and organised around clearly defined purpose. At the end of 19th century, the spirit of voluntarism filled the missionary agencies which demonstrated the Western values of "activism, do-goodism, and manifest destiny" (Bosch 2007: 332). These Protestant mission agencies were commonly known as "faith missions", and the most famous of these was the China Inland Missions (CIM) which was founded by J. Hudson Taylor in 1865. At this time, an urgent call was made to young men and women to bring the gospel to millions of people in China and other distant countries. In this period, the new societies also adopted a radical orientation in the volunteerism principle. Many people were challenged to go without financial support, which made them "heroes of faith to some people", "fools" to others, and "fools for Christ" to yet others (Bosch 2007: 333). A sense of urgency filled these believers who felt that there was no time to waste and that they had to travel out to proclaim the gospel at the greatest speed. So many of them went with little preparation or training, though some of those recruited were well educated. This situation also led to some weaknesses of the faith mission movement, namely, a romantic notion of mission; the view of individual freedom to make personal choices, an obsession with saving people's souls before Judgement Day, and a lack of understanding of the cultures and religions of the people to whom they have gone. These missionaries were almost entirely dependent on the charismatic personality of their leaders and a very low view of the church. Nevertheless, the movement had its strength. An example was Hudson Taylor of the CIM. The headquarters, or what the missionaries called their "home base", was not in London, Berlin, or New York, but in China, India, and Thailand. The missionaries lived in "mission stations" which were separate from the local peoples, but in the midst of their communities. They ate food, wore clothes, and lived like the locals as much as they could. The emphasis was not on doctrinal differences but the simple gospel of salvation through Jesus Christ (Bosch 2007).

The motives of the missionaries were mixed, depending on their Christian denomination. There were mixed beliefs about how their social engagement was related with their preaching of the gospel. However, in general, the belief was that in serving those plagued by suffering and poverty, they were serving Christ. In addition, across the 19th century and the first part of the 20th century, the motives and theology of the Christian missionaries were to civilise the minorities, in a sense to "prepare" them for salvation and entry into the Kingdom of God by meeting their basic needs first (Wilfred 2014b). The missionaries felt that the indigenous people could not receive the gospel until their basic needs such as hunger were met first. The missions of the Christian workers also involved the liberalisation of the minorities from the bondage of the surrounding society. At the same time, the rise of the Social Gospel movement in the West had an impact on the social engagement of these missionaries. Where previously the preaching of the gospel in the First Awakening had to do with spiritual aspects of repentance and salvation, in the Second Awakening, it involved an additional concern with the social implications of the situation of the people, such as industrialisation, migration, prostitution, and workers. Christianity also played a significant role in introducing Western medicine and medical care into Asia. Peter Parker, from the American Board of Commissioners for Foreign Mission (ABCFM), established the Canton Hospital in China 1835 to provide medical care, train a new generation of local doctors and nurses, and become "agents of modern medical care and social hygiene" (Wilfred 2014: 6).

Therefore, early Christian missionaries to China were participating in social engagement in its broadest terms, i.e. to convert the Chinese people to Christianity and, ultimately, create a new kind of society which is ideally conceived from the perspective of Christian principles (Cohen 1963; Spence 1984; Leung 2007). This has been a persistent theme in the story of Christianity in China. Throughout the 19th century, both Catholic and Protestant missionaries arrived in greater numbers in China through both trade and forceful means, leaving lasting impacts (positive and negative) on the development of modern

China in the early 20th century (Lutz 1971; Smith 1985; T'ien 1993; Liu 2008; Wang 2008). Positive impacts include the setting up of schools, universities, orphanages, hospitals, vocational training institutes, and other charitable organisations that aimed directly at improving the lives of the Chinese people:

> Besides evangelism, missionaries often pioneered in social reform and services and helped introduce modern medicine and education as well as Western culture. Missionary institutions such as St John's University, Yenching University, and Xiang-Ya (Hunan-Yale) College of Medicine and Hospital, as well as Young Men's Christian Associations (YMCAs) that dotted the urban Chinese landscape, became ensuring symbols of the contribution of Protestant missions to China's modernization.
>
> (Lian 2010: 6–7)

Christian social engagement in China was viewed by some people with suspicion as it was considered to be a Western penetration and domination in the country. However, the many marginalised ethnic minority communities welcomed the missionaries (Harrell 1995; Diamond 1996; Han 2000; Hirono 2008). The ethnic minority, the Hua Miao, for instance, welcomed the missionaries who helped them gain greater mobility through the educational services the missionaries provided. In China, where literacy and education were important to gain access to the positions in the state bureaucracy, the work of the missionaries in providing education was an important empowerment for the marginalised. Through the work of the missionaries in translating the Bible into the languages of the minorities, it gave the latter respect and confidence in their languages and cultures. Due to the oppression that they suffered, these minorities found security in the missionaries, whether it be poverty alleviation; education; medical or business work that the missionaries started in their communities. The missionaries were also responsible for the changing women's socio-economic conditions in China, through their anti-foot-binding movement and education for girls. In the 19th century, in particular for rural women and women of lower and middle class, the work of Christian women missionaries among them offered them dignity and self-worth.

The arrival of Christianity has also been an important factor in many sociocultural upheavals and changes in China (Cohen 1963; Teng 1971; Han 2000; Liu 2006). These include the rupture of existing social structures as new converts rejected traditional Chinese social and religious norms, and the provocations of missionaries through their denigrating of local cultural practices. Anti-foreigners sentiments surfaced in China periodically and peaked in the Boxer Rebellion of 1900. The rebels attacked Chinese and foreign Christians, resulting in 230 Western missionaries being killed, of whom 189 were Protestants, and 79 were from China Inland Mission. In particular, two events in China fuelled anti-foreign attacks on missionaries and their social engagement: the Opium Wars and the suppression of the Boxer Rebellion by the combined Western imperial forces. On 1 October 1949, the Communist Party, under the leadership of Mao Zedong, proclaimed the founding of the People's Republic of China. Within a year, thousands of foreign Protestant and Catholic missionaries were expelled from China. The missionaries' support of the Kuomintang Nationalist Party and anti-communism sentiments also hampered their social engagement as they were seen as opposing Communism's atheist ideology. At this time, the number of Chinese Christians had reached 3 million Roman Catholics and 75 million Protestants (Aikman 2003).

Christianity in contemporary China

In contemporary China, many Chinese people no longer consider Christianity a "foreign" religion or a tool for Western imperialistic expansion. Some even regard it as a prestigious religion that symbolises modernity and cosmopolitanism. Yang's (2005) study of conversion to Christianity in urban China depicts the crucial contexts for the rising numbers of new converts in the 1990s. This was happening in the cities where China's experience of the globalising market economy and the resulting impacts were most acutely felt. Increasingly number of urban residents, disenchanted with communist ideology after the Tiananmen violence of 1989, while also experiencing anomie due to rapid social change, began to embrace Christianity as a viable source of religious and moral certitude. Many of these new converts viewed Christianity positively as signifying liberalism, democracy, modernity, and cosmopolitanism. Among these newly minted Christians were members of an emerging elite group in Chinese urban society, consisting of successful businesspeople, university students, and professionals (Gao 2005; Cao 2011; Kang 2016). The substantial social, cultural, and economic capital acquired by the highly educated Christian professionals and intellectuals has in turn endowed them with greater organisational and mobilisation capacities in the pursuit of their religious goals. In the cities these days, many independent Christian groups are renting commercial premises for conducting their religious activities, when this is often illegal. Christians' increasing willingness to take an assertive negotiating position vis-à-vis the authorities was clearly seen in the incident involving the Shouwang church in 2001. The Shouwang church members, after being forced to vacate their original premises, held outdoor services to publicise their displeasure with the official handling of their case and staked out a prominent presence in the public sphere. The overall picture we get from most of current research of the urban churches is thus one of rapid growth and vitality (Gao 2005; Yang 2005; Kang 2016).

In contrast, detailed anthropological studies of Christianity in the rural areas paint a more ambivalent picture. Over the last two decades, many Christian village communities have witnessed the re-opening of local churches and much greater freedom to practise their faith (e.g. Liang 1999; Ng et al. 2005; Lim 2009a; Huang 2012). As China opened up to the world from the early 1980s onwards, village religious life, even in seemingly remote areas, has been increasingly shaped by translocal and transnational processes. In the book *God above Ground*, Lozada (2001) examines how the church of "Little Rome", in a predominantly Hakka village in Guangdong province, has been rebuilt with flows of funds from the Hakka diaspora. This was accompanied by a resurgence of religious faith in the 1980s and 1990s. In the villagers' desire to pursue "development" and "modernity" in the new market economy, Catholic rituals have played a significant role in integrating other aspects of the villagers' engagement with transnational processes such as economic migration, consumption, and nation-state building, as part of their interpretation and experience of being "modern" in the contemporary world.

Similarly, in his research in Wu village in the Gansu province, Huang (2017) notes how both the official Catholic and Protestant churches had initially benefitted from the reforms and new religious policies in the 1980s. However, since the late 1990s, the village churches have experienced a marked decline, precisely because of the village's deepening integration into translocal and transnational flows. One of the most important factors behind the decline is economic migration, as the young in the village, especially men, join the millions of migrants from other parts of China to move to the cities in search of jobs and better life. The result has been the gradual hollowing out of the rural Christian community. According to Huang's informants, there were almost no new converts in the five years since 1997, and the churches these days are no longer as vibrant as they used to be. Huang (2017) observes that the numbers of people attending church events are always far lower than what the church leaders claim as the size of the local Christian community. To Huang, the church seems like an "Old Folks' club" or a "Women's club".

Conversely, Protestant Christianity, in particular, has attracted huge numbers of new believers in both rural and urban areas. As Lian Xi notes in his book *Redeemed by Fire,* one important reason is the transformation of Christianity "from an alien faith preached and presided over by Western missionaries into an indigenous religion of the masses" (Lian 2010: 2). The rise of popular Christianity—contrasted with Western denominational churches and Christianity of the elite social strata—has continued to shape the essential character of popular Protestantism which is embodied by the house churches in China. It has "fostered a new form of Messianism in a country where millenarian movements have been one of the few possible ways to channel the aspirations and the discontent of the masses" (ibid.: 16). There has also been intricate interplay between state actions and the institutional features of Protestantism behind the rise of Protestantism in Post-Mao China.

Sun (2011) identifies six key institutional features of Protestantism in China, namely, zero-sum evangelism, congregational structure, insistence on church autonomy, a polycephalous structure, glorification of martyrdom, and global support network. In themselves, these institutional features are unable to fully explain the rapid expansion of Protestantism in China. The role of the state, specifically the unintended effects of its actions during Mao and post-Mao eras, shaped the crucial sociopolitical context which was conducive for Protestantism to gain a stronger foothold in China. On the one hand, a series of state's anti-superstition and anti-feudalism campaigns between the 1950s and the late 1970s undermined the traditional normative and institutional orders of Chinese popular religion that had historically strongly opposed Christianity at the grassroots level. On the other hand, the state's pursuit of market-oriented economic development during the post-Mao era has resulted in relative weakening of political control in the local society. Local officials were much more interested in demonstrating their capabilities in spurring economic development than controlling religious activities. In addition, the understaffing of relevant bureaucracies such as the local Religious Affairs Bureau meant that implementation of religious policies was not effectively carried out. Hence, a combination of the institutional features of Protestantism and the (unintended) state actions has resulted in the rapid rise of Protestantism over the past four decades. As the following chapters will demonstrate, Chinese Protestant Christians' increasing engagement with social media has further enabled them to spread their faith rapidly. It has further enhanced their application of Christian beliefs in their work and everyday life, which further intensifies their mindset that their Christian beliefs can influence the larger society, thus bringing about social change subtly and slowly.

What has happened in China mirrored the developments in the broader Asia region, where the interaction between Christian and Asian societies has led to fundamental and profound changes, both positive and negative, for both Christianity and the societies concerned. As Felix Wilfred (2014a) notes, the "interaction between Christianity and Asian cultures and societies, however, is only at its beginning" and Christianity's impact in Asia will continue to be felt in "intellectual revolutions, religio-cultural confrontations, and social conflicts". Our book is thus a story of a continuing saga, in that it explores the interaction between Christianity and a major Asian society that leaves profound legacies in both the parties.

Significance of study

An important avenue for Christians to be what they term "change agents in society", or vehicle of social change, is the community development work they engage in, particularly those of FBOs. While it might seem in contemporary China that religion is primarily doing the bidding of the party-state in religion's philanthropic activities and development work, historically, religion had often been in the forefront of philanthropic and charity work. Laliberté, Palmer, and Wu (2011) note that many Chinese religious associations had been engaging in philanthropic and charitable activities services well before the Christian missionaries introduced the modern notions of philanthropy and charity to China in the late 19th century. One reason is that traditional Chinese religions' universalistic conception of compassion and benevolence dovetails with philanthropic ideals. Another reason is that religion had traditionally been an important part of Chinese people's social, economic, and public life. Religious beliefs and rituals were critical to people's pursuit of personal physical and spiritual well-being; they were also essential for the imperial state for its legitimation and the integration of the empire.

In the revolutionary decades following the fall of the Qing before the founding of the People's Republic, the communists had branded charities as "anti-revolutionary forces", ostensibly helping the needy but, were in fact, institutions that had emerged from the structures of a bourgeois society. Foreign charities and philanthropic activities were denounced as instruments for Western imperialists to shape the Chinese people's social and cultural norms (Luova 2017). After the CCP came to power, Western "bourgeois" religious charities were expelled along with their foreign staff, while local self-help groups based on clan and lineage networks were denounced and discontinued as legacies of Confucian feudalism. The new communist regime attacked non-state charities and aid networks, religious or non-religious ones, as part of its broader assault on the private property and other foundations of the "old society". Motivated by its totalitarian impulse, the party-state considered the existence of any private or non-state charitable organisation as an affront to its self-styled paternalism (Hsu 2008). Foreign Christian missionaries and clergy were expelled from the country, while most of the charitable organisations or denominations ran by them were forced to either shut down or merge under the state-sponsored national Protestant and Catholic churches. To this day, there is "in principle no space in official Chinese policy for an independent civil society, and therefore no space for independent religious associations" (Madsen 2010: 61).

The economic reforms over the last four decades in China have unleashed a torrent of market forces in China. This has resulted in the phenomenal rise in the standards of living for many of the country's citizens. At the same time, new social problems and fault lines have emerged, such as rising income inequality; heightening social tensions; environmental degradation, rampant official corruption; forced expropriation of farmers' land, mass migration of workers from rural areas to major cities, and mounting cases of food safety violations. Concerns over the state of the citizens' moral well-being had surfaced, even in the early days of the "reform era". Commentators questioned if the unleashing of the market forces in society had negatively impacted on social relations and morality (e.g., Hanafin 2002; Ci 2009; Osburg 2013). Relatedly, the question of whether religion can contribute to the "moral reconstruction" (*daode zaijianshe*) of contemporary China has preoccupied many ordinary citizens, scholars, policymakers, and religious leaders, in recent years (Shue 2011; Liang 2014; Yan 2014; Fisher 2017).

In this book, we use the notion of social suffering to refer to "an assemblage of human problems [that] results from what political, economic, and institutional power does to people and, reciprocally, how these forms of power themselves influence responses to social problems" (Kleinman et al. 1997: ix). In other words, the concept of social suffering describes "an interpersonal ground of suffering" that analytically situates a person's experience of suffering in a larger web of interpersonal relations and current societal issues. Social suffering is a general condition that may impact on different socio-economic classes in different ways. The poor and disadvantaged groups experienced social suffering most acutely due to their lack of access to resources to ameliorate the negative effects (ibid.)

There exist varied conditions that give rise to social suffering, involving health, welfare, legal, moral, and religious issues (Kleinman et al. 1997: ix). Partly in an effort to find appropriate responses to widespread social suffering in China, the question of how religion may contribute to the "moral reconstruction" of contemporary China has preoccupied the minds of some scholars, policymakers, and religious leaders in recent years (Shue 2011; Fisher 2017). In the context of the People's Republic, the Communist government's efforts to include religions' activities in its agenda for nation building was, therefore, not contrary, but, an implicit part of religions' overall mission to serve the larger society. In addition, it provides these religions a window of opportunity to legitimise their faith to the government and society. Through such social engagement, they could show that their beliefs and religious activities have a relevance socially.

In recent years, there have been significant shifts in how the party-state views and regulates the charitable and philanthropic sectors (Wu 2016), and this includes non-government organisations that engage in development work. In the context of rapid social and economic changes that resulted in heightened social sufferings, the party-state began to encourage—even as it faced intense internal debates and criticisms—the development of the charitable sector, partly to implement its social welfare policies, and partly to cultivate communitarian values and mutual aid as a response to rising social ills. To the party-state, being charitable became one of the qualities of a civic minded citizenry (Luova 2017: 138). Fällman (2010) has proposed an intriguing interpretation of the effects of the party-state's renewed interest in the mobilisation of religion for its own agenda, calling it "reverse opium theory". He argues that the party-state was trying to use religion "as 'opium' in a way that Lenin strongly condemned, i.e. to calm people and create stability and 'harmony'". This meant that religion "should contribute to the reduction of contradictions, legitimize party policies and in reality, make the population passive to reduce opposition on social and political issues". However, an unintended consequence could well have been engendered, which is the strengthening of faith among the country's citizens, and creating favourable conditions for the emergence of the rights protection movement (*wei quan yundong*), with strong links with Christian groups (Fällman 2010: 967, 969).

In the last three decades, some Chinese intellectuals have reflected and written on how Christianity might provide solutions to some of the pressing social and moral issues in contemporary China. These intellectuals include those who do not formally embrace the faith in confessional terms but are, nevertheless, immensely concerned over Christianity's role in shaping China's future. Wielander (2009) examines the activities of Christian intellectuals in house churches and their implications for China's democratisation process. She finds that Christian public intellectuals' activities could potentially serve as "bridges" between theory and practice, rural and urban divide, social class divisions, as well as China and the world. This would, in turn, contribute to a broader civil society activism that seeks to achieve a deeper democratisation in China. Since the late 1990s, a group of public intellectuals have emerged for whom Christianity is both a personal faith and source of their political ideals. Christian intellectuals, such as

Wang Yi and Yu Jie, are prominent human rights activists, whose activities have been met with harsh responses from the authoritarian party-state. Others have looked to Calvinism for inspiration to engage with the state and society. They accomplish this by formulating a theology of constructive dialogue (Chow 2018: 20–21). Yang (2010: 197–198) has argued that, for Christianity to establish itself even more firmly in the Chinese culture, a Chinese Christian theology has to be developed, based on the empirical work that details the Christian communities' contemporary interpretation of their faith. To this end, some leaders and theologians in the official Three-Self Patriotic Movement have reflected critically about the role of the church in a rapidly changing society that is fraught with tensions and faced with huge challenges. Some have proposed a "Theological Reconstruction" to enable the Christian church to maintain its relevance in society, through greater social awareness and engagement (Wang 2001; Wickeri 2007).

Qin's (2019) study of the Evangelicals in both the house churches and Three-Self Church shows a noticeable trend among Chinese Christians towards greater sociopolitical engagement since the 1980s. According to him, the Chinese church has experienced three trends of evolution from the 1980s to the 2010s. In the first trend, there has been a shift among house church Evangelicals away from a privatised faith of Christian piety towards a more open engagement with society. The second trend involves the Three-Self Church and Evangelicals' movement away from theological reflections on Christianity and Chinese culture to a more society-oriented positioning. Third, Evangelicals in both the house churches and Three-Self church have come to view deeper social engagement as being essential to the practice of Christianity in China.

On the house church front, prominent leaders such as Jin Mingri, Yu Jie, Wang Yi, and Sun Yi have advocated a deeper engagement in the public sphere through involvement in charitable and philanthropic projects, development of a public theology, and, in some cases, advocation for political democratisation. Examples of such social engagement causes involve highlighting the widespread social suffering and the civil authorities' failure to solve many social issues. Jin Mingri evokes the church's cultural mandate (*wenhua shiming*) to address these issues through education, charity, and social services. Yu Jie exhorts Christians who had hitherto been practising a privatised, inward-looking form of Christian piety, to face the wider society and consider social engagement as an integral component of the Christian faith. Meanwhile, Sun Yi, influenced by Neo-Calvinism, likens the church as a "city set on the hill" whose openness and integrity were to showcase the moral standards for the wider society. For the contemporary Christians in China, one important way in which members of the unregistered churches participate in the public arena in a highly restrictive environment is to demonstrate acts of patriotism (Vala 2018). Protestant pastors may exhort and encourage members to participate in patriotic prayers, public relations, and charitable and social work programmes (Koesel 2014). While doing so, they are not seeking to challenge the authority of the party-state. On the contrary, they seek to strengthen and grow their churches. They also aim to cultivate positive images across the state and society. Many of these Chinese clergy members are looking for effective means to achieve their goals and protect own interests while negotiating in a restrictive political environment. This *cri de coeur* for the church to play a more active role in the public sphere has also been echoed by prominent leaders of the official Three-Self church such as Wang Weifan and Wu Weiqing. Comparing Wang and Wu's approaches, Qin (2019: 270) comments that:

> Generally speaking, Wang draws his motivation from traditional Chinese culture, while Wu derives a burden from the masses' interest in society ... Wu focuses his interest on social issues closely related to ordinary people. Regarding serious social problems, Wu employs Christian teachings and refers to faith in Christ as the solution to problems [and] is burdened with problems of moral deterioration and social injustice.

In recent years, with the influx of the highly educated professionals and city dwellers, the dominant Protestant evangelical tradition of religious piety and aversion to politics and social engagement has given way to a more variegated position towards social awareness and political activism (Yao 2011: 67–68). For example, some Protestants have embraced human rights activism and regard the quest for social justice, religious freedom, and political reform as integral to the practice of the Christian faith. Others have established strong connections with overseas churches and human rights organisations which share the same social and political agenda and have often acted as spokespersons of China's house churches, in the international media. However, the majority of the house church congregations tends to take the middle ground approach of being more engaged in social issues, while refraining from political activism and direct confrontation with the party-state. Some prominent political activists who have converted to Protestantism show a diminution of prior political activism. Being evangelical and fundamental in their beliefs, these former political activists have become more focused on proselytising and saving souls, and much less concerned with calling for democratic political change (Wright and Zimmerman-Liu 2013).

For the Catholics, religious social engagement in the forms of charities and philanthropic activities has long been an important part of their faith as encapsulated in the Church's social gospel (Wilfred 2014b). Especially significant is the expression of *caritas*, one of the Church's seven virtues, defined in the Aquinian terms as neighbourly love that unites humanity with God. Even in times of tightened reins over religion in the post-Maoist era, Catholic charities have continued to provide much needed social welfare services in areas such as health care, education, and the care for the disadvantaged and marginalised segments of the population. Many of these charities were affiliated with the official China Catholic Patriotic Church and worked closely with local government officials and organisations.

Given the importance of the social gospel for the Catholic Church, scholars have queried whether the Catholic Church could contribute to the development of civil society in China through its social engagement. This is especially the case for the so-called "underground" Church, with its occasional demand for greater religious freedom (Leung 2005; Chan 2013). In his classic study on China's Catholics, Madsen (1998) argues that while the Church and its members have historically engaged in many charitable activities, the official Church, as a whole, is more inward looking. Its members (many of whom live in Catholic-majority villages) eschew participation in the public sphere and social movements to push for reforms. In short, despite the gradual opening up of spaces for religious social participation, the Catholic Church in China, as an organisation, is more a conservative, than a reforming, force in China.

Madsen's argument has stimulated further research on the question of whether the Catholic Church is institutionally capable of contributing to the development of civil society and broader reforms in China. We shall here draw on the important findings of Chan's research which was conducted in the city of Wenzhou in Zhejiang province. Adopting an institutional approach, Chan examines the changing state-religion relationship between the local governments and Catholic Church in Wenzhou since the beginning of the reform era. Chan has found that the Wenzhou authorities' management of the local Catholic Church has moved from a period of lessening control in the 1990s to the current situation whereby there has been a tightening of regulation and suppression of the influence of the Church. This phase "was marked by the government's campaign to remove crosses from the rooftops of churches and demolish church buildings in Zhejiang Province under the policy of 'Three Changes and One Demolition Action' (meaning it would change the old residential areas, factories and villages which are surrounded by expanding cities by demolishing illegal buildings)." They did this with the ultimate aim to reduce the influence of the churches in the region.

Over the last two decades, the Church in the Wenzhou diocese, like in many places in China, split into various factions among the clergy and the laity. First, the division of the Catholic Church into an official church and an underground church led to different opinions among the members of the clergy and the laity on how the Church as a whole should engage the government and how much it should advocate for greater religious freedom as part of a broader sociopolitical engagement. Second, Chan found that, among the clergy in the official Church, some have chosen the path of collaboration and negotiation with the party-state, while others have preferred the path of resistance and confrontation. Crucially, the different paths taken have resulted in different outcomes with regard to religious freedom:

> Among the four factions in the Catholic Church, the choices of *accommodation* and *confrontation* have proved to be deficient. Those who chose accommodation had to work for the CCPA, which was isolated from the majority of the clergy, while those who chose confrontation had no legal status and they could not administer the church openly. On the contrary, the choices of *negotiation* and *resistance* have proven to be more desirable. Those who chose negotiation could administer the church openly with their legal status and they could deal with government officials in negotiations, which led to the latter making concessions. If government officials refused to concede, the clergy could resist the local government in its implementation of policies

> and regulations. It is in these choices of negotiation and resistance that the Catholic Church in Wenzhou has been able to expand its limited space of religious freedom.
>
> (Chan 2016: 15, italics added)

The research by Chan and other scholars in recent years further revises Madsen's original argument. In the last three decades, the Catholic Church has been an active participant in certain aspects of social change (e.g. improving the lives of the physically and mentally handicapped, providing better medical care for AIDS and leprosy sufferers, quality childcare and education to the poor). Certain segments of the official and underground Church are also seeking to expand the space of religious freedom in the country through negotiation with, and sometimes resistance of, the government. In Wenzhou, until a few years ago, the so-called Boss Catholics played an active role in church planning and development while negotiating with government officials. And unlike the Protestant entrepreneurs who have mostly sought to cultivate a cooperative relationship with the local government officials (Cao 2011), the Catholic entrepreneurs seemed to have utilised their business and problem-solving skills to resist church–state relations (Chan 2016: 13–14).

Beyond civil society

Existing studies mainly focus on the activities of formal religious organisations in civil society and their interactions with the state, such as charity and philanthropy (e.g. McCarthy 2013; Carpenterand den Dulk 2014; Wu 2016; Weller et al. 2017). This civil society approach has provided useful insights into the broader sociopolitical contexts that enable religious groups to participate in China's social change, especially through philanthropic and charitable activities. In their case study of Tzu-Chi, a transnational Buddhist NGO, in transnational volunteerism in China, Lee and Han (2016) argue that FBOs are playing an increasingly active role in Chinese civil society. They show how Tzu-Chi, with extensive volunteer networks and vast ability for resource mobilisation, was able to play a crucial role in relief work and welfare provision in the transnational Malaysia Airlines MH370 incident. In recent years, the service gaps that have emerged between state and market have created a structural opportunity for FBOs to actively engage in a wide spectrum of welfare and relief provisions in China. A policy change in 2012 has further encouraged the involvement of FBOs in welfare provision. Under the new policy, FBOs enjoy tax exemption status and other benefits when contributing to the country's welfare system (Lee and Han 2016: 2371). Some FBOs have embraced the position that considers disaster relief work, development projects, and charitable activities an integral part of religious cultivation. At the same time, FBOs, like Tzu-Chi, often seek to present themselves as apolitical. This is to establish trust and goodwill with various governments and other civil groups in order to facilitate greater ease of operations for these FBOs. Wu (2016) has shown how the party-state's practice of "adaptive governance" combined with a "responsive religious field" has facilitated the rise of religious groups' participation in philanthropic and charitable activities. As a result, such religious groups have experienced increasing bureaucratisation and professionalisation, while their lay members construct moral selves based on "universal values of love, reflect admiration of rationalized organization. They also draw on, and extend beyond, earlier socialist moral discourses of 'doing good deeds.'"

Nevertheless, the last few years have witnessed the Chinese authorities' stepping up of their efforts to monitor religious groups, including Christian groups, which are not officially registered with the authorities. For instance, the Chinese government is very much aware of Catholic Church's role in the downfall of Communist governments in Eastern Europe. In fact, Pope John Paul II (1920–2005) encouraged the Church in his native country, Poland, to be involved in anti-communist opposition. It was because of the Church's role in political changes in Eastern Europe, Latin America, and elsewhere that the Beijing took a stronger position towards Roman Catholicism, which it viewed as predominantly anti-Communist. The government has recently passed tougher laws and regulations to circumscribe religious activities and direct various religions to adhere more strictly to the party-state's agenda. This has proceeded in tandem with the broader crackdown on China's nascent civil society since Xi Jinping came to power and exert more forcefully the Communist Party's authority over all aspects of life in China, including religion. In April 2018, the government-sanctioned China Christian Council and the Three-Self Patriotic Movement published a highly significant document, "Protestant Five-year Plan for Chinese Christianity", on the so-called Sinicisation of Christianity. An excerpt notes that:

> The Sinicization of Christianity is not only an objective requirement for the development of the church in China itself but also an *ardent expectation of the Communist Party and the government.* In recent years, the party and the government have repeatedly stressed the importance of doing religious work properly to fully implement the party's basic policy on religious work, to persist in the direction of Sinicization and to actively guide religions to adapt to socialist society.
>
> (https://www.ucanews.com/news/protestant-five-year-plan-for-chinese-christianity/82107. Accessed 23 April 2018)

In contemporary China, when the existence of civil society is empirically and theoretically in doubt, how are individuals and groups who are motivated by religious concerns and values able to contribute to social change? Our book tackles this question by offering a new approach that examines domains outside of civil society, where religious groups and believers actively seek to embed their religious values in their social settings. The book suggests looking beyond the common approaches of examining religious organisations' philanthropic and charitable activities and their mobilisation in civil society. It highlights the importance of examining the non-obtrusive and non-antagonistic activities which interact with controlling state institutions (e.g. Klandermans 1988; Katzenstein 1990). Specifically, we analyse the non-obtrusive and non-antagonistic religious social engagement of Chinese Christians in three arenas: social media, community development, and the workplace. By religious social engagement, we mean the efforts of religious individuals and groups who are seeking to address social issues by engaging in activities which may, or may not, involve widespread and coordinated mobilisation efforts. By examining such activities which are not normally considered part of civil society activism and coordinated mobilisation, this book demonstrates how Christianity continues to experience rapid growth in the context of the deepening political authoritarianism, curtailment of civil society, and tightening reins over religion by the authorities.

Methods

Our methods of collection of data for this book comprise in-depth, semi-structured, and structured interviews. Between 2013 and 2017, we also engaged in periods of fieldwork, totalling eight months in mainland China alone, and the rest of the time, in Hong Kong and Singapore. Our research respondents comprised 45 Chinese Christians who are based in mainland China (Chengdu, Kunming, Shenzhen, Wenzhou), Hong Kong, and Singapore. The respondents in Mainland China and Singapore were all mainland Chinese, consisting of lay Christians and members of the clergy who belong to both official and independent Catholic and Protestant churches. We recruited these respondents through snowball sampling, starting with the Chinese Christians we know personally in these three countries. For many years, one of us had been a volunteer with a foreign Christian development NGO which has been engaging in poverty alleviation and medical and educational projects in southwestern China for two decades. We conducted in-depth interviews with five past and present volunteers and full-time workers at the NGO. Data was also collected from participant observation in the NGO's activities and its official publications. We also conducted online participant observation in Chinese Christian groups on various social media platforms (e.g. QQ, WeChat, Facebook). The political sensitivity of the topic meant that we had to establish high levels of trust with our informants and ensure strict confidentiality. The Chinese Christians agreed to us joining their groups in social media because one of us is a Christian and has been involved in teaching the mainland Chinese Christians in a theological college and church in Singapore. Another of us was introduced to the Catholic and Protestant clerical informants in Mainland China and Hong Kong through personal acquaintances in these two places.

Organisation of the book

In Chapter 2, we present our main theoretical approaches and the various concepts we utilise for analyses in the subsequent chapters. We first discuss the theoretical approach of viewing religion as an everyday practice and how this form of conceptualising religion is appropriate for analysing Christianity and social change in the context of China. This is followed by theoretical elaborations on the concepts of atheist secularisation and unobtrusive social engagements. This chapter highlights how these concepts are used in the subsequent chapters on religious use of social media, pursuits of "holistic development", and the practice of Christianity in the workplace.

One of the most remarkable social trends in China in recent years is the explosion of mobile internet and social media usage. In Chapter 3, we use the concept of intercontextuality to analyse the processes in which the Chinese Christians integrate spiritual and religious capital on social media, such as WeChat, QQ, and Facebook. Through what we call networked transmission of religious values, social media enabled our Chinese Christians respondents to discuss different aspects of their lives such as religious practices and activities related to daily lives and work. At the individual level, this amalgamation of religion with daily activities often blurs or ignores the institutional distinction between the "religious" and "non-religious". While neither openly discusses "sensitive" issues nor mobilises on social media, many of our respondents nevertheless wish to disseminate Christian values through online social networks. We end this chapter with a discussion of the limitations of using social media for the transmission of religious values in China.

In Chapter 4, we analyse how Chinese evangelical Protestant employees view work and the workplace from a religious perspective, and how they seek to influence the broader society through the workplace. While existing China-focused studies have mainly examined the experience of the Christian business elite (Chan and Yamanori 2002; Cao 2011; Lee, McCann and Yuen 2012; Tong 2012), in this chapter, we enquire into the experience of the employees. Working in predominantly non-Christian and secular workplaces, these employees discursively construct a distinction between their own Christian work ethos and that of their non-Christian colleagues. They regard the workplace as an arena where Christian evangelism, the perceived moral decline of contemporary society, and the supposed solution to the crisis are entangled. For these evangelical Protestant employees, the cultivation of personal piety and engagement in the subtle proselytisation in the workplace is not only a matter of saving souls but also transforming the moral fabric of society.

Chapter 5 presents a case study of an international Christian NGO, GMV (a pseudonym), which has been working in China for decades. Given the Chinese government's increasing strict regulations on the activities of civic and religious groups, especially foreign ones, how can foreign Christian groups such as GMV pursue their aims of transforming Chinese society, spread Christian messages, and seek new converts? To answer this question, we demonstrate how ideological disguise shapes the discursive practice of development of both GMV and the party-state in their interactions with each other. For the officials and bureaucrats of the party-state, the practice of ideological disguise involves, first, the insistence on the "secular" or "non-religious" dimension of the work conducted by the religious NGOs. At the same time they choose to downplay or publicly ignore the fact that the volunteers and workers may be religiously motivated. Community development entails the improvement of local infrastructure, literacy, healthcare provisions, skills training, and other competencies and capabilities that are not ostensibly related to religious ideology and matters. For religious NGOs such as the GMV, ideological disguise involves downplaying, or even publicly disavowing, the religious messages and intent in their community work as they interact with an officially atheistic government.

In the concluding Chapter 6, we summarise the major arguments in our book. We reiterate the need to go beyond the civil society approach to understand the role of religion in ameliorating social suffering through social engagement and changing moral and behavioural norms in China. While not denying the fact that the party-state continues to actively monitor and bend religion to its will to achieve its goals, we argue that religion often slips outside the arenas in which they are circumscribed. Much of existing scholarship has demonstrated that religious organisations and individual actors have done so by negotiating, accommodating, or collaborating with, and sometimes resisting, the authorities. We argue in this book that there is another story which has not been adequately told. This is the story of how religion is infused into society through popular technological culture and the workplace, and this is facilitated by religious actors who find connections with a global discourse of holistic development.

Notes

1 The purpose of this section is to set the context for the subsequent discussions in this book and hence not an exhaustive survey on this subject. From among a voluminous body of work, see e.g. Harnack (1961); Winter (1994); Bosch (2007); MacCulloch (2010); Jenkins (2011); Wilfred (2014); Hovey and Philips (2015); Akanbi and Beyers (2017); and Gutterman (2018).

2 The discussion of missionary societies in the next few paragraphs is drawn primarily from the classic work by Bosch (2007).

2 City on a hill

Atheist secularisation and religious social engagement

In this chapter, we examine, from various theoretical perspectives, the intriguing phenomenon of religious revival in China, under the government of an authoritarian Communist Party. We may be surprised by the phenomenon, if we agree with the classic formulation of the secularisation thesis. A common trend can be seen from observations drawn from Christianity's development in most Western European societies in the first half of the 20th century, and the strong form of the secularisation theory, as exemplified in Bryan Wilson's *Religion in Secular Society* (1969). This trend supposedly suggests that, as society modernises, religion will become an increasingly private and individual affair, and, concomitantly, lose its public significance, or become less significant in people's lives. For example, the advent of Protestantism in Europe brought about the idea of religious understanding that it is a personal matter. Peter Berger vividly described this process as one in which religion loses its "sacred canopy". Meanwhile, increasingly, ecclesiastical properties and institutions have been expropriated by non-religious authorities for secular ownership and use. In addition, historical data show decreasing numbers in church attendance, which seemed to suggest that, at the individual level, religion is also losing its attraction for many people.

Atheist secularisation

Wallace and Bruce (1995) further elaborate on the orthodox model of secularisation in relation to modernisation theory. They analysed how the main features of societal modernisation may result in "the diminution of the social significance of religion" (1995: 11). First, according to them, increasing social differentiation brings about the rise of specialised roles and institutions that are able to deal with the specific functions which were formerly carried out by religious institutions. Examples include the provision of education and medical care. Second, Bruce and Wallace argue that the process of societalisation has contributed to the demise of the public role of religion as life has come to be organised, not by the local community, but by the more encompassing modern nation state. In other words, society has supplanted community as the locus of individual's life. The two processes of differentiation and societalisation have led to the demise of a single overarching religio-moral system. Simultaneously, it conditions the rise of multiple competing religious and moral conceptions within society. The third feature of modernisation that contributes to the decline of religion's social significance is rationalisation. By that, Wallace and Bruce refer to the "pursuit of technically efficient means of securing this-worldly ends", or what Weber calls the "disenchantment of the world". In other words, the technical and scientific rationality has prevailed over the substantive rationality of religion in the public life of a modernising society.

If we accept this secularisation thesis, we will be surprised by the situation in which religion in China has not disappeared from both private and public spheres in China, even though the Chinese Communist Party has directed intensive modernisation efforts since it took power in 1949. No doubt, the features of modernisation can be witnessed in China, as elsewhere in the world. While liberal-democratic governments often maintain a neutral stance towards religion, the Chinese government is not neutral. Instead, it is influenced by Marxist materialistic social evolutionism, and it believes that religion will recede as modernisation proceeds (Madsen 2010: 59). Religion in China has not faded from both public and private lives, confounding the prediction of the secularisation theory. This begs the question: to what extent is the concept of secularisation useful in explaining the religious situation in China? In other words, has secularisation happened in China? We suggest that rather than disregard the term completely, it is useful to rethink the secularisation concept in the more specific contexts of China and the Communist political systems (Ngo and Quijada 2015).

With China becoming a neo-totalitarian state, Ji (2015) argues that "since 1989, the Chinese communist regime has been characterised by an unprecedented fear on the part of ideological self-confidence". Partly in response to potential threats to its authority in the post-Tiananmen era, the ruling CCP's religious policy "is driven by purely instrumentalist reasons of Power, rather than by cultural convention or an ideological legacy" (Ji 2015: 95). China has indeed undergone processes of secularisation, but not in the way that is expounded by the secularisation thesis which has developed primarily from the experience of Christianity in Western liberal democracies. While China has undergone modernisation like many other countries, this secularisation is not characterised by a separation of religion and state. Ji utilises a juridical approach to argue that secularisation in China entails the secular authority's appropriation of religious property (both material and symbolic) to serve its political agenda. Rather than being characterised by a strict separation of church and state, secularisation in China comprises the state mobilisation of religious resources for its own ends. Ji referred to China's case as "secularization without secularism" (2015). In this sense, secularisation is typified by a process of ongoing power struggles between the secular state and religious forces. Therefore, it is not unilateral and irreversible. Secularisation is a process that can be slowed down, maintained at current levels, or reversed if religious forces are able to exert their power relative to the state's authority. For example, since the founding of the People's Republic, the CCP has sought to exert control over various religions. It legally recognises five official religions by forming national associations for each of these religions. In the case of Buddhism, since the founding of the PRC, the CCP has appropriated various Buddhist symbolisms, mobilised its clergy, and utilised its monasteries for its political campaigns and other secular objectives. The government also established the Buddhist Association of China (BAC) as a national organisation that oversees the all aspects of Buddhism in China. Over the years, while its main aim is to bend Buddhism to its will, the government's secularisation efforts have resulted in the institutionalisation of Buddhism as a resource-rich, church-like entity with legitimate public and social roles. This leads to the unintended consequence of the BAC's acquisition of political, symbolic, social, and economic capital to become an authoritative entity. It is thus often able to negotiate with the state in its own terms.

Koesel's (2014) interest-based framework also focuses on the power struggles between state and religion. First, Koesel argued that mutually beneficial interactions between religious groups and authoritarian regimes create the favourable conditions for the former to flourish and make an impact in the public sphere. Authoritarian regimes, such as China and Russia, may seek to bolster their legitimacy by co-opting religious institutions and symbolism. Religious actors may wish to engage the state in more practical issues, such as legal recognition and attainment of funding for their social welfare services. In the case of China, McCarthy (2013) terms this the "repurposing of the state". Second, such kind of interactions can be most obviously seen at the subnational level, as in the example of local officials who invite religious groups to participate in service and social welfare provisions. Third, historically, there are many examples of religion–regime cooperation in both Russia and China. An important implication of the study of subnational interest-based religion–regime relations is that it helps to explain the durability of contemporary authoritarian regimes.

Another approach to Ji's view that China's secularisation has proceeded without secularism is to conceptualise it as a process that results from a specific kind of secularism, namely, atheist secularism (Ngo and Quijada 2015). At the ideological level, Communist state-sponsored atheism requires an antithesis, namely, religion, in order to define itself and mobilise the population for social transformation. Therefore, in China, the CCP "needs" religion as its "Other". This "Other" forms part of its own political imaginaries and efforts to shore up its legitimacy. Over several decades, the CCP has constructed various meanings of "religion" for its own political projects, through ideological, legal, and administrative means. While this effort has indeed been profoundly impactful on the state regulation of religion and the understanding and practice of religion in China, such constructions never fully determine the nature of religion in the country. In other words, there are ideological, conceptual, and legal gaps that allow for alternative constructions and, hence, practices of religion in China. At times the government has sought to suppress religion, such as during the militant atheistic period of Mao's rule. On other occasions, it reverts to an atheism that tolerates religion in both the private lives of the citizens and the public arena. Conversely, the state also mobilises religion for its own political and ideological agenda. Therefore, although China's Constitution enshrines the principle of religious freedom, religion in China has never been a wholly "private" affair, at least not in the ideal-typical liberal sense in which citizens have the freedom to engage in religious affairs without any (state) coercion. The China party-state, through its religious policies and political activities, has always sought to control and manage religion. As Ngo and Quijada (2015: 14) argued, "Communism did not allow a separation of church and state, since the state sought to occupy all social space".

Meanwhile, we must also not fetishise that the state is a monolithic entity. Rather, it consists of different levels of administration, different departments, and multiple individuals (Eng and Lin 2002; Chau 2005). It is an agglomeration of actors that formally organise themselves into institutions in their practice of governance. State entities may sometimes work together for common aims, or may come into conflict with one another, because their actions and agenda do not cohere. Occasionally, they have sought religion's eradication, such as during the militant atheism phase of Maoist period. At other times, they accommodate, support, or harness religious forces to achieve their political goals, such as their current more pragmatic and accommodative stance (Leung 2005). The party-state's discursive practice of official atheism, as a form of secularism, is productive in the generation of ideas, concepts, and practices of "religion" in society. At the same time, we must also be aware that such discursive practice can evolve and revise over time, giving rise to shifting ideas, concepts, and practice in different historical periods. In this sense, in the Communist Party's ideological practice of its atheist secularism, religion has always been "public" affair and not a separate "private" domain of the citizens. Hence, the important issue is the actual nature of publicness of religion, as construed by the party-state as well as the believers. This is because both these groups interact and negotiate with each other over the extent to which the party-state can, or should, legitimately intervene in the religious life of the citizens. In addition, the religious believers can, or should, legitimately participate in the social, cultural, and political processes (i.e. public life) of the nation.

The above review of atheist secularism and secularisation sets the societal and political contexts for our analysis of religious social engagement in the rest of the book. While we largely agree with the literature cited above, our research findings strongly suggest that religious groups do not only carry out their activities and pursue their agenda in the legitimate spaces carved out by party-state policies. They also creatively utilise both discursive and non-discursive means to create their pathways in a more subtle manner. This leads to our argument that we should also examine the unobtrusive social engagement of religious groups.

Unobtrusive religious social engagement

In light of the discussion above, we can reformulate our empirical question in this way: Under China's atheist secularisation, how has Christianity continued to experience rapid growth in an increasingly restrictive political environment, especially with heightened government efforts to curtail Christianity's rapid rise? Another related, broader issue is the link between religion and social change in China. There are two main approaches of dealing with this issue in the existing scholarship. The first approach examines social movements that involve the mobilisation of religious groups and individuals. The second approach analyses the role played by the Christian elites, especially the Protestant intellectuals, in the demand for more social and political freedoms. Both of these approaches are linked to the discussion of civil society in China.

The civil society concept has recently received much attention by scholars of Chinese affairs. The challenge for China scholars lies in the applicability of the concept of "civil society" to the Chinese context, where the state still exerts enormous control and influence over both public and private life. Under such conditions, it would be erroneous to view civil society as a space that is largely separated from the state or family (Ma 2006). Drawing on Kang and Heng's (2008) idea of "graduated control", Wu and Chan (2013) demonstrate that the relationship between the state and NGOs is very much influenced by the latter's business nature. The party-state exerts its most stringent forms of control on groups which are mainly involved in advocacy work relating to political, religious, ethnic, or other sensitive matters. A consideration of the features of China's civil society is therefore essential in order to understand both the opportunities and constraints religious agents face as they seek to play a more prominent role in society through development work, philanthropy, and charitable activities.

Generally, the civil society approach has been fruitful in helping us understand the broader sociopolitical contexts that have enabled religious groups to participate in the process of social change in China. In addition, it offers insights into how religious groups have been playing an important role in forging an expanding social space for themselves and other non-religious groups. As Carpenterand den Dulk (2014) note, religion "often plays a vital role in helping citizens 'mediate' between their own interests and the competing interests of the state". In China, religion "has played a role in an emergent Chinese civil society, notably its fostering of countless congregations and social service organizations" (Carpenterand den Dulk 2014: 7). From their research on educated, upper-middle-class Christian converts, Ma and Li (2014) argue that these Christians tend to integrate their faith with social and political affairs, and are more likely to engage with the public sphere as a socio-economic group. They seek to offer alternatives to the official ideology of the ruling Communist Party.

However, in recent years, as the party-state tightens the reins over civic groups (including religious groups) and curtails civil society activism, how are individuals and groups who are motivated by religious concerns and values able to precipitate social change? Our book addresses this question by examining the non-obtrusive and non-antagonistic religious social engagement of Chinese Christians. By religious social engagement, we mean the efforts by religious individuals and groups which are engaging in discourses on social issues which may or may not involve widespread and coordinated mobilisation efforts. Some of these activities may be conducted in ways that are non-obtrusive and non-antagonistic in terms of the religious groups' interactions with controlling state institutions (e.g. Klandermans 1988; Katzenstein 1990).

Much research on social movements have focused on how groups endeavour to change aspects of society through contentious tactics in order to challenge dominant powers and authorities. There is a need to also understand how social groups may strive to change society through unobtrusive and consensus-based tactics. Kucinskas (2014) identifies three main ways of doing this. The first way is through discursive politics. A classic example is the effort by feminist Catholics to create new discursive space to stimulate reflections and reforms in order to promote greater inclusivity, without directly challenging the existing authority structures of Catholicism. In the following chapters of the book, we discuss how Christian informants strive to create a discursive space for their participation in social transformation. They do this by downplaying or eschewing the distinction between the "religious" and "secular" domain, even when the party-state and other non-Christian secularists seek to enforce such a distinction. They concomitantly embrace the widely held discourse in China (by both the party-state and the general public) that much of the social problems can be attributed to a "moral malaise" that pervades contemporary society. In this case, the discursive politics is illustrated through our Christian informants' effort to legitimate their religious social engagement through, namely, development projects, networked transmission of values on social media, and transforming workplace culture.

The second way, as identified by Kucinskas, is through creating a "state within a state", or "burrowing into" secular institutions. In this approach, religious groups could use uncontentious tactics to infiltrate various secular fields, bypass the official state, and create a "parallel society" which is underpinned by their religious ideology. In this regard, our informants who are working for the international Christian NGO constantly try to showcase their "professionalism" in medicine, education, social work, etc., as they engage state representatives and other societal actors in "holistic" community development projects. In the secular workplace, an important way for Christians to exert their subtle influence is by aligning Christian values with those of business and interpersonal relationships. This is often achieved with the ultimate aim of promoting the "right values". It is hoped that these values will ultimately diffuse throughout the workplace and wider society. In both cases, Christian NGO workers and business employees, who are motivated by their strongly held religious values, are able to occupy the same discursive space as "Others".

The third unobtrusive strategy is to assimilate and blend. Drawing upon research on how a Buddhist-inspired movement diffuses into popular Western culture, Kucinskas shows that contemplatives often use "insider access and knowledge to translate and adapt Buddhist culture so that it blended into institutional cultures in targeted organizations" (Kucinskas 2014: 547). For example, these contemplatives try to demonstrate how meditation practice is beneficial to employees' mental health and productivity levels while deliberately concealing the Buddhist ideology behind the practice. In this way, supporters of meditation are able to establish points of convergence between two cultures without incurring suspicion and negative feelings among those who may be sceptical of Buddhism. This method of unobtrusive religious social engagement is seen in our case study of the GMV, the international Christian NGO. Like many other FBOs working in multicultural, multireligious and sometimes ideologically hostile environments, GMV's approach to "development" is very much aligned with prevailing international development groups. They embody values such as "holistic development", "sustainability", "community", and "participation" in their development projects across diverse countries and cultures. Crucially, this is also the approach which is favoured by different governments, ranging from liberal to authoritarian ones like China's. Such convergence of discursive practices between FBOs, like GMV, and the Chinese government at various levels and regions enables the GMV to pursue its work even as most of its informants framed their motivation in religious terms.

Unobtrusive religious engagement: three cases

Networked transmission of values

In this book, we conceive media and religion as being deeply embedded in Chinese culture. Using the concept of everyday religion and social media as popular culture, we wish to examine how Chinese Christians construct, negate, question, transcend, or reinforce institutionally defined social domains such as "religion", "the secular", and "politics", as they embark on creating online religious networks. According to the China Internet Network Information Center, as of December 2015, there were 620 million mobile internet users in China, with around 90% of them using mobile phones to access the internet. The weekly average online duration per citizen in 2015 was 26.2 hours. In our recent research trips to China, the communication tools that were most preferred by friends and research collaborators were mobile apps such as QQ and WeChat (both are part of Tencent, the technology firm), which are two of the most widely used social media sites that are accessible via smartphones in China. It is significant that the widespread use of mobile internet has taken place in tandem with the state's strict surveillance and censorship regimes. China's banning of global social networking sites like Facebook, YouTube, and Twitter, and the denial of access to many foreign websites, have resulted in the rapid growth of Chinese firms which are offering similar services. A commentator observes that "many Chinese netizens would not distinguish between social media and the Internet itself", such that "the Internet is social media and vice versa" (Crampton 2011). In short, social media and (mobile) internet have become popular culture in China. The rise of mobile internet and social media has allowed Chinese people around the world to communicate with one another for a wide range of purposes. While the government may be busy monitoring and censoring websites, simultaneously, ordinary Chinese users of the internet (the netizens) and smartphones are using different ways, both legal and illegal, to circumvent government restrictions in order to connect with one another within and outside of China.

Some years ago, Helland (2005) proposed a widely discussed distinction between "religion online" and "online religion". The former refers to information about religion that is accessible via computer-mediated networks. In China, many Christian organisations, both official and unofficial ones, have their own websites with information about their activities and various aspects of the Christian faith, such as, key beliefs, history, evangelism, and links with other Christian groups outside China. Such examples include ccctspm.org (中国基督教网站), chinacatholic.org (信德网), and gospeltimes.cn (福音时报). The last site, gospeltimes.cn, allows readers to share its articles and videos via 56 social networking sites. Some independent churches even have their own regular online publications (e.g. *Aiyan*, *Xinghua*). "Online religion", on the other hand, refers to the various ways in which religious faith is practised over these networks. Nowadays, this distinction increasingly breaks down as most websites offer believers both information and opportunities to practise their faith, such as sharing of Bible passages and prayers in the forums, watching of video streams of sermons, engaging in debates over theological or pastoral matters, and plugging into translocal and transnational networks of Christian communities via hyperlinks. The hugely popular video sharing site Youku has many videos and programs with Christian themes, such as the *Daily Song* (每日一歌), which forms an integral part of a Christian spiritual cultivation. The interactivity that the internet affords its users can facilitate the formation of online religious communities where members share information, hold debates, provide mutual support, plan activities, etc. (Brasher 2001).

Ethical workplace

In the sociological literature, the relationship between religion, spirituality, and work was famously analysed by Max Weber in his *Protestant Ethic and the Spirit of Capitalism*. As is well known, Weber starts with a discussion of Luther's interpretation of the notion of vocation, or "calling" (*beruf*), as entailing a spiritualisation of worldly activity (Frey 2008). Luther's interpretation of the calling directly led to the Calvinist notion of inner-worldly asceticism, which is the key religious orientation that Weber identifies as the basis of the "spirit of capitalism". Contemporary advocacy on spirituality and religion in the workplace can at least be traced to the Faith at Work movement that had first emerged in Europe and the United States in late 19th century. Then, an increasing number of Christians tried to foster a closer integration of faith and work, in order to ensure that religion remained relevant in addressing the issues of the workplace and the wider society. Miller's (2007) historical study of the Faith at Work movement highlighted the influential role played by the Protestant clergyman Walter Rauschenbusch in articulating a social gospel and exhorting Christians to participate actively in, and transform, the business domain. Rauschenbusch's key message was that through a transformation of the self, business, and the workplace, religion could continue to be a potent force in a rapidly secularising society. The movement contributed to the rise of post–World War II Protestant ecumenical activity that emphasised the ministry of the laity, especially in their respective occupations. The insecurity, constant change, and intense pressure associated with many modern secular occupations have ironically stimulated a quest among many workers to turn to spirituality and religion, in order to find meaning in their lives (Miller 2007).

In the Catholic Church, Pope Leo XIII in 1891 issued the encyclical *Rerum Novarum* (The Condition of Labour), urging a closer assimilation of religious values and actions, in all aspects of a Christian's life, including the work life. The Second Vatican Council (1962–1965), again, stressed the importance of the laity in supporting the Church's evangelical mission in their workplaces. Many Christians have indeed aspired to adopt a "holistic" approach in practising their religion. They reject the notion that spirituality and religion should be confined to one's "private" domain and not be entangled with one's occupation. Popular books on business leadership and management, such as Bruce Barton's (1925) *The Man Nobody Knows*, advocate taking Jesus as a role model for business leaders. Rick Warren's (2014) *The Purpose Driven Life* is a good example of how Christian writers continue to advocate making religion directly relevant to everyday life and work, and how many lay Christians believe this to be immensely important to live a meaningful and fulfilling life.

Some past research has looked at the creation of a favourable work culture and business leadership. For example, some research has shown that the cultivation of spirituality in organisations might enhance employees' well-being, instil positive attitude towards work, and create a more amiable workplace (Mitroff and Denton 1999; González-González 2018). Employees' spiritual well-being is found to have positive impacts on their morale, ability to cope with stress, motivation levels, and productivity at the workplace (Sass 2000; Benefiel 2005; Duchon and Plowman 2005; Fry, Matherly, and Quimet 2010; Chen and Yang 2012). In Sri Lanka, a study finds that when business leaders embrace spirituality in the workplace, they also strive towards self-actualisation and are more concerned with ethical decision making (Fernando 2002). In view of the potential benefits of workers' integration of religion, spirituality, and work, Hicks (2003) argues that business leaders should create a pluralistic and supportive environment for employees to achieve faith integration at the workplace.

Some scholars who are adopting a more critical approach have highlighted instances of the senior management's "symbolic violence" on employees who are working towards integrating faith in the workplace. Drawing on Bourdieu's critical sociology, Kamoche (2012) argues that the top-down imposition of organisational spirituality is a new way for firms to manage and discipline their employees. In Malaysia, for example, the country's push to develop products for its Islamic economy has resulted in the adoption of sharia (Islamic legal codes) by some companies to shape their workplace culture (Sloane-White 2011). Executives in these firms seek to develop "personnel sharia" that govern employees' ethical values and moral principles, as well as "corporate sharia", which are based on the Quran and the Hadith, for commercial and managerial activities. In such Islamic workplaces, piety and Islamic subjectivities are not just solely a matter of individual choice, but are also shaped, monitored, and enforced by a sharia-raised corporate culture.

Other studies have investigated the relationship between the expression of religious identity and the risk for perceiving or experiencing discrimination at the workplace. For example, studies have overwhelmingly shown that Muslims and Jews are more likely to perceive discrimination at the workplace in the United States and the UK, whether or not the issues of religion ever emerged at the workplace (Mythen, Walklate, and Khan 2009; Ghumman and Jackson 2010; Scheitle and Ecklund 2017). This has prompted some believers, especially Muslims, to deemphasise or hide their religious identity, either at the workplace, or when seeking employment. Thus, while research has uncovered some benefits of incorporating religion and spirituality into the workplace culture, other studies have also shown that expressions of religiosity and spirituality could often lead to stigmatisation, conflict, tension, distraction, and discrimination in the workplace (Gregory 2011).

Most studies on religion in the workplace are conducted in countries where governments are relatively tolerant of religion, and not in places where religion is tightly regulated, such as in China, the former Soviet Union, and Vietnam. Thus, while some researchers have argued that businesses should promote a better integration of religion, spirituality, and work, this measure is difficult, or even impossible, to be implemented in certain countries with strict secularist policies (e.g., France) or with governments that are ideologically atheistic (e.g., in Communist party-states). Although China's constitution allows for religious freedom, religion in China is not a "private" affair, at least not in the liberal sense. By this token, citizens lack freedom to engage in religious affairs that are free from state monitoring and coercion. The Chinese party-state, through its religious policies, has always sought to control and manage religion. It imposes strict regulations on where religious practices might be conducted (Leung 2005; Laliberté 2011). In China, it is illegal for citizens to practise religion in the workplace. Hence, in this book, one of our aims is to examine how believers view work, and the possibility of bringing their religious faith to the workplace, where it might be a part of the religious "gray market" (Yang 2006).

Scholars who have studied religion and work in China mostly focused on the business elite or the Christian entrepreneurs. One earlier study examined how China's entry into the World Trade Organization has provided opportunities for the Chinese Christian entrepreneurs to exert their influence in both economic and spiritual affairs in China (Chan and Yamamori 2002). In recent years, many so-called "Boss Christians" in Wenzhou also strove to shape the Chinese nation in both material and spiritual terms (Cao 2013). They hoped to exert a moral influence on society by letting Christian values guide their business activities, interpersonal relationships, and philanthropic projects. In effect, they are melding a form of elite Christianity with the ideals of spiritual nationalism. Lee, McCann, and Yuen (2012) found that conducting business in China has a negative impact on ethics among some Chinese Christian business leaders. Meanwhile, for the business leaders, a Christian corporate culture is highly conducive for sustaining Christian witness. In a study by Tong (2012) on overseas Chinese Christian businesspeople in Shanghai, he found that personal piety serves as the foundation of business ethics. It guides their dealings with Chinese officials, clients, business partners, and ordinary workers. In their study on trust among Protestant entrepreneurs, Tong and Yang (2016) found that Chinese Protestant entrepreneurs want to be more trustworthy and trustful of others, and some of them think that a major religion like Christianity would lead to better moral behaviour.

The representative studies cited above underscore the importance of gaining an in-depth understanding on how religion impacts the meaning of work, workplace behaviour, and work ethics. In broad terms, therefore, this chapter examines how Chinese evangelical Protestants seek to integrate their faith in the workplace. We take faith integration to mean "the attempt of Christians in the workplace to think, feel, and act in ways that reflect their identities in Christ" (Stansbury 2015: 23). With past research on religion (especially Christianity) and work in China, that are mostly focused on the business elite, our attention is on the experience of the Chinese Christian employees who work in enterprises that were mostly established by non-Christians. While our analytic focus is on the individual level, it is contextualised in the relevant organisational and societal environment. We examine the meaning that evangelical Protestant workers attribute to their work, from the viewpoint of religion, and how as individuals they seek to express their faith in environments that often prohibit the overt practice of religion. The question of how Christians, who belong to the professional class, view work and express their religiosity in the workplace is one that deserves serious study. As a class of people as a whole, they are economically, politically, and culturally influential in contemporary China. This is also the social class for which work or occupation is a crucial defining element of its members' personal and social identities (Bourdieu 1987; Lamont 1992; Bottero 2004). Our analysis on believers' attitude towards their work and colleagues, and how they seek to influence the wider society, will contribute to the scholarship on religion and social change in China.

Holistic development

The devastating Sichuan earthquake in 2008 is often mentioned, in scholarly accounts and the NGO circles in China, as a pivotal event that saw the widespread mobilisation of civic groups, including religious NGOs, to deal with the humanitarian challenges resulting from the earthquake. This incident has also prompted renewed academic and societal-wide reflections on the significance of religious organisations in contemporary Chinese social, economic, and political life. Historically, many Chinese religious organisations have been actively engaged in philanthropic and charitable activities (Smith 1987, 2009; Weller 2006; Laliberté, Palmer and Wu 2011; Tan 2012). When the Chinese Communist Party came to power in 1949, it aggressively sought to dismantle both religious or non-religious non-state charities and aid networks. This was part of its broader assault on private property and other institutions of the "old society". It denounced self-help groups based on clan, lineage, and religious networks as legacies of feudalism. At the same time, foreign charities, philanthropic activities, and non-governmental organisations were accused of being instruments for Western imperialists (Luova 2017). Motivated by its totalitarian impulse, the party-state considered the existence of any private or non-state charitable organisation as an affront to its self-styled paternalism (Hsu 2008).

However, since the early 1990s, there have been significant shifts in how the Chinese government views and regulates the charitable and philanthropic sectors, including the non-governmental organisations that engage in development work. In the context of rapid social and economic changes, the party-state began to encourage the expansion of the charitable sector, partly to implement its social welfare policies. The other purpose is to cultivate communitarian values and mutual aid in response to rising social ills. To the party-state, being charitable has become an important part of civic mindedness (Luova 2017: 138). Crucially, over this period, China has been increasingly entangled with the global development discourse and practice, and interacting with international development organisations and NGOs that form part of the global civil society. Significantly, in 1987 the Civil Affairs Bureau initiated efforts to develop "community services". This initiative created opportunities for civic groups (including religious groups) to be involved in providing social welfare services and "community building" (*shehui jianshe*) (Zuo 2015). Meanwhile, the government also mobilised the social sector, including religious groups, in its community services projects.

Consequently, in recent years there has been growing scholarly attention on religious organisations' involvement in charity and philanthropic activities in China. Such studies tend to fall under either the resistance model or the accommodation/interactional model. Under the former model (e.g. McCarthy 2013), analyses tend to focus on how religious charitable and philanthropic activities take place in the context of resisting—despite—the state's highly restrictive and often punitive religious policies. The resistance model provides insights into the workings of unequal power relationship between the China party-state and civic actors. This model shows how the party-state is often in the commanding position of shaping the country's social, political, economic, and cultural domains. Notwithstanding this, some civic groups are occasionally able to counter or circumvent the government's machinery, and contest its agenda and actions. One weakness of this model is that it often portrays civic organisations as mainly reacting or responding to the party-state's agenda. The model attributes high levels of agency, authority, and legitimacy to the party-state which it may not necessarily possess. An underlying, and often unstated assumption of this model is that the relationship between the party-state and civic organisations is fundamentally fraught with contention, opposition, and power struggle. Whether this is actually the case is an empirical question that needs investigation, rather than assumed a priori from the outset of analyses. Relatedly, analyses using the resistance model may miss or downplay the possibility that some civic groups and the party-state may have overlapping interests, agenda, priorities, and values. These parties may also agree broadly on certain actions and modes of intervention to address particular social issues.

In contrast to the resistance model, the accommodation/interactional model examines how religious organisations and the party-state organs are often mutually co-opting or accommodating in their desire to work together in the provision of social good. Typifying this approach is Wu's (2016) study on how Buddhist and Protestant organisations have undergone bureaucratisation and professionalisation in the context of the state's assertion of its authority over religious groups, and its demand that the latter demonstrate positive contributions to society. For some Buddhists in China, the endemic social sufferings they witness in society motivate them to actively practise compassion in their daily life and engage in voluntary works as a form of this-worldly spiritualism. Doing good works in society is understood by the Buddhists as part of practising gratitude while also allows for the accumulation of good karma necessarily for spiritual cultivation (Kuah-Pearce 2014). These social actors often work alongside local government officials and state-related organisations. Meanwhile, they also acknowledge the practical need to work with party-state entities to achieve the desired outcomes of their social interventions. However, the accommodation/interactional model tends to overlook or inadequately address the important issue of the wider discursive contexts that influence the desire of civic organisations and the party-state authorities to work together. It also overlooks how the actors involved refer to and incorporate the same discursive frameworks to motivate, rationalise, and legitimate their activities vis-à-vis their national and external constituencies. For example, why would both party-state actors and religious groups emphasise "holistic development" in their community development and poverty alleviation efforts? Why are norms such as "professionalism" and "sustainability" embraced and highlighted by these different entities which are often ideologically opposed to one another?

What is inadequately addressed in the two models discussed above is the broader global contexts of development discourses and practices, especially how the global initiatives on "community", "holistic", or "balanced" development have created a space for religious groups to participate in development work in a country that still maintains tight control over religion and NGOs (both local and foreign). Such new paradigms concerning development which are circulated by global civil society; international development organisations, and multinational governance institutions (e.g. the U.N.) have exerted profound influences on national development policies. In addition, they shaped the interactions between civic groups and government entities. This chapter focuses on a case study of GMV to demonstrate how an FBO's ability to work in China cannot be explained solely in reference to its religious values and motivation, or the internal social and political conditions of China. We argue that a comprehensive account of the work of religious development organisations in the country needs to include an examination of the prevailing global discourses on the ethics of development practice. Such ethics has shaped, and been shaped by, the involvement of FBOs, national governments, global civil society, and global discursive practices of development (Lim 2020). There are four components in the global field, each of which is relativised and defined in terms of the other three, thus allowing for

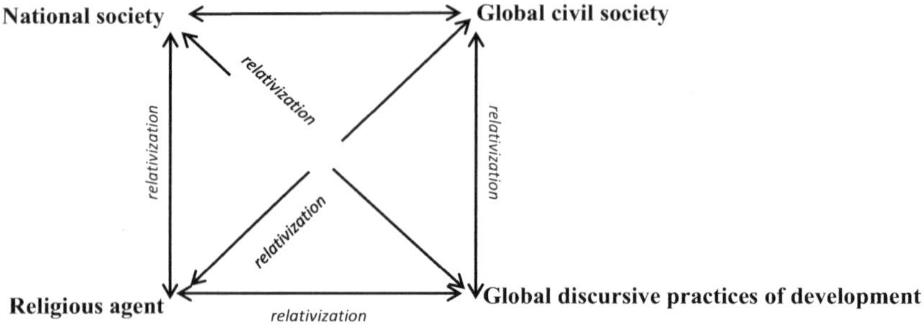

Figure 2.1 Religion and development ethics: the global field (Lim 2020).

a dynamic framework for analysis. Crucially, the interactions between these four components condition the changes that occur in each of them (ibid.). We shall elaborate on these four components below.

In Figure 2.1, the *religious agent* refers to any religious institution that actively engages in activities which are related to humanitarian effort, religious giving, and development (broadly defined). Using the global field framework, we examine how GMV's mode of and justification for its activities are "relativised", or defined in relation to prevailing global discursive practices of development. Meanwhile, a religious agent, such as GMV, is in discursive and operational interactions with the state and other similar civic groups in the national society. Moreover, the legitimation of these discourses and practices is done through the processes of negotiation, collaboration, and contestation in the domain of transnational civil society. How should development be pursued, and for what ends? What are the measures and criteria for adequate development? These are issues over which nations and organisations which are involved in philanthropic and charitable work, including religious groups, are continually negotiating with one another.

Global civil society is a domain where national societies, international organisations and groupings, and non-governmental organisations (including religious agents such as GMV) interact, negotiate, collaborate, and contest with one another over appropriate global norms and means to set standards for the pursuit of development and well-being. The *national society* analytically comprises two elements: the state, and national civic groups. First, the state stands in a problematic relationship to a particular religious agent via its promulgation and enforcement of policies, rules, and regulations which pertain to charitable, philanthropic, and humanitarian work. At the same time, it interacts with, and responses to, transnational social movements, and prevailing or emerging *global discursive practices of development* (i.e. the dominant normative discourse of development and associated practices). The second element of *national society* comprises the civic groups. The crucial consideration is whether a civil society has emerged that allows civic groups and non-governmental organisations (including faith-based ones) to engage in developmental efforts, humanitarian work, and charitable causes.

In applying our global religious development model, we need to emphasise the fluidity of the Chinese state relationship with the Christian international NGO. China is faced with changing policies in its political, social, and economic landscapes that affect changes to the relationships between religious international NGOs and the government. There is a constant need for religious international NGOs to legitimise its work with the state as well as evolve the nature of their community work. First, the Chinese government needs to exert its sovereignty and seeks to work towards autonomy in providing social services to their own people. Subsequently, the government has taken over many religious international NGOs' work and turned them into their official social service. In fact, the Chinese government has taken over the youth hostel work of GMV and made it their official social service. This shows a growth in the Chinese state's social service sector in that it is willing to assume the social responsibilities for the marginalised. From the Christian perspectives, it means that the NGOs have to evolve their orientation and goals to adapt to the changing state's policies and goals. The objectives of the NGOs need to transform to one of partnership with the local Chinese volunteers so that they could legitimise their presence and work.

Everyday religion, the social sacred and ideological disguise

In the field of religious studies, scholars have been sharpening their focus on how believers practise religion in their everyday life, often without paying much attention to what the institutional religion might say regarding dogmas and orthodoxy (McGuire 2008; Schielke and Debevec 2012; Ammerman 2013). In this book, we use the concept of lived religion to examine how Chinese Christians negotiate, transcend, as well as maintain and enforce institutionally bounded domains. These domains include "religion", "the secular", and "workplace" which form the subjects of their social interactions as they forge Christian communities. Some scholars (Hall 1997; Woodhead 2013; Cochran 2014) have argued that, for many religious believers, there are no clear boundaries between religion and public and private lives. In their everyday practice of religion, people may ignore institutionally constructed boundaries that separate social life into different domains. They often do so with little attention to institutionally defined religious dogmas and orthodoxy. For many of our research respondents, this is the case. At the same time, their practice of religion in the everyday life disrupts the state's attempt to regulate and manage religion by confining it within officially demarcated "religious" domain, such as in officially approved religious sites and organisations. However, the respondents do this in ways that will not draw the attention of the government.

When Chinese Christians are practicing religion in their everyday lives and engaging in unobtrusive religious social engagements, many of them are, at the same time, seeking to promote and embed Christian values in the wider society.

In part, they are motivated to do so as they want to evangelise to other non-Christians, and also to act to ameliorate prevailing social ills. However, these Christians are not acting alone. There are other social actors who are pursuing the same goals of social reforms but are motivated by different religious, non-religious or political values. Consequently, we propose the concept of "social sacred" to describe these common goals and ideals.

The social sacred refers to an agglomeration of ideals which are widely shared among different social groups which are striving for attainment of common good of society. The social sacred concept builds on the new sociology of morality that does not assume a societal-wide consensus on morality and internalisation of moral values among social actors, institutions, and groups (Hitlin and Vaisey 2013). We do not presuppose a universal consensus on moral meanings as the key underpinning basis of social solidarity. Neither are we adhering to a Parsonian functionalism that tends to collapse morality into moral norms and moral consensus. Such a move presupposes a singular moral system and conceptualises morality as closely linked with conformity (Parsons and Shils 1951; Spates 1983). Hence, our notion of the social sacred does not entail complete agreement among social groups over its exact meaning and content. In addition, social groups and state actors may or may not agree with one another over the means to achieve social sacred.

Therefore, the specific contents of the social sacred may emerge from contestation and negotiation between differently positioned groups and institutions (with differential access to power and resources) over what is good or bad; desirable or non-desirable; right or wrong, and worthy or unworthy for society. In this formal approach, the meanings and content of social sacred are changeable. They exist at multiple, cross-cutting, and competing levels, and not so much in society in general (e.g. Inglehart and Baker 2000; Lamont and Thévenot 2000; Smith 2003; Lukes 2008; Abend 2011; Fligstein and McAdam 2012). The social sacred can comprise a host of related ethical notions, such as *suzhi* (embodied quality), civic mindedness, honesty, kindness, love, reciprocity, community development, faithfulness, and integrity. For our Christian respondents, these virtues are interpreted through a Christian lens. For an officially atheist party-state, these very same virtues or social goods have "humanistic", "secular", and non-religious bases. We further propose using the concept of ideological disguise to analyse how the pursuit of the social sacred is possible, even among ideologically opposed social groups. Ideological disguise refers to the efforts undertaken by social groups to tactically de-emphasise or "hide" their foundational ideologies in public engagements, in order to attain long-term strategic goals.

The concepts of social sacred and ideological disguise, thus, enable us to analyse and explain how religious groups and individuals, as well as representatives of an officially atheistic party-state, seemingly work together for the attainment of social goods and civic virtues (i.e., social sacred), even when the different participants may not necessarily share the ultimate sources of those ideals. For instance, in the chapter on "holistic development", these two concepts allow us to analyse how both the party-state and a Christian NGO may agree with one another on the social value of "development", which enables them to work together in various development projects. At the same time, both sides differ in terms of the ultimate values that underpin and shape their development goals. The party-state's goals of development are ultimately political and economic in nature, whereas the goals of development of the Christian NGO are not only economic but also religious. The practice of ideological disguise, therefore, allows both the party-state officials and religiously motivated NGO workers to publicly affirm and collaborate in order to attain shared social goods and virtues, while still adhering to their respective strongly held ideologies or ultimate values.

To some degree, Christians engaging in community development in parts of China can overcome state restrictions on religious activities by using social media (cf. Travagnin 2017). With greater ease of communications made possible by social media, these Christian groups can communicate the needs of impoverished communities in China to international NGOs. They can execute transborder management, planning, and execution of community development work in these Chinese communities through internet-enabled networks, without having to meet physically all the time. They form international teams to conduct medical, business, and educational training programmes in these communities. With such communications, which are made possible by social media, they can introduce expertise knowledge which would otherwise be unattainable to these Chinese rural areas. In the Chinese Christians' engagement with social media, they also brand their faith in accordance with impressions of modernity. This shows that Chinese Christians embrace change and respond readily to modern technology as tools of both their practice and spread of their faith.

In addition, a set of common Christian values and ethics about work galvanises many of these Christians, in and outside China. In turn, these Christians believe that they are influencing the Chinese communities with their Christian values in their selfless and unconditional conduct of their professional work in the communities. These Christian values, which they hope to transmit to the Chinese communities, have both social and spiritual attributes. These values embody the spiritual Christian doctrines about work which shape personal character and, ultimately, transform social interactions and relationships. In the next three chapters, we present more detailed discussions on how Chinese Christians practise Christianity as everyday religion and also engage in unobtrusive social engagements on social media, in community development work and the workplace.

3 Bonds of perfectness

Networked transmission of Christian values

Rise of the internet and social media in China

One of the most remarkable social trends in China in recent years is the explosion of mobile internet and social media usage. Internet connections became available to the average urban consumer in China after 1996. By 2003, China had the second largest internet users in the world, next to the United States. Social acceptance was found to be high among the Chinese internet users (Zheng 2008). According to the figures released in 2018 by the China Internet Network Information Center, there were 880 million internet users in China. The rise of mobile internet and social media has allowed Chinese people around the world to communicate with one another for a wide range of purposes. Social media usage has become part of popular culture in China. A commentator observed that "many Chinese netizens would not distinguish between social media and the internet itself", such that "the internet is social media and vice versa" (Crampton 2011). Traditional media, like the newspaper, are no longer the first source of news for people as news spreads across different websites before they are released by traditional media. In short, social media and (mobile) internet have become popular culture in China. This can be seen by the widespread usage of the microblog platform, Weibo, and the mobile chat app, WeChat. In 2017, WeChat alone had around 494 million individual users in China and hit 1 billion user accounts worldwide (Yuan 2018). In addition to its social messaging function, WeChat is also a wildly popular platform for e-commerce, mobile payments, and blogs. The phenomenal success of online retail service providers, such as Alibaba and Taobao; online gaming, and Twitter-like social media, such as Sina Weibo, has resulted in the penetration of the internet and mobile services into all domains of Chinese social, cultural, economic, and political life. China's engagement with social media has surpassed many other developing and developed countries. This has a profound impact on social relations and cultural change in China.

While the government is busy monitoring and censoring websites, ordinary Chinese users of the internet (the netizens) and smartphones are stepping up efforts to connect with one another. It is significant that the widespread use of mobile internet has taken place in tandem with the state's strict surveillance and censorship regimes. The emerging rich online culture created by the Chinese internet users reflects the "freedom ultimately granted to them by the central government or agencies, and are not an expression of the Chinese government's inability to control the internet" (Herold and Marolt 2011: 2). A good example was when the government shut down the internet in Xinjiang after clashes between Muslim Uighurs and the Han Chinese in the summer of 2009. A well-discussed feature of the internet in China is its "quasi-separation" from the rest of the World Wide Web (ibid.). There are four methods employed by the central government to achieve this. The first involves the establishment of the "Great Firewall of China" (GFW) that "exists as a multi-faceted and ever-changing system of both national as well as local rules, combined with technical limitations caused by the set-up of the internet infrastructure" (Herold and Marolt 2011). As an example, the speed for accessing and loading websites hosted overseas is considerably slower compared to local sites. The system also allows the government to easily block access to specific websites and domains that it deems "undesirable". The second method that the central government employs to control the internet is the ISP-enforced blacklisting of specific words. If someone were to search for sites containing words as "Falun Gong" or "Tibetan independence", the connection between the person's computer and the ISP would be cut. Third, the government can choose to bend multinational technology companies to its will by controlling the degree with which these companies are able to operate in China's domestic markets. For example, Google largely exited China's internet search market after refusing to submit to censorship efforts by the Chinese government. The final method which the Chinese government uses is the control of individual computer users, such as requiring the users to register before being allowed to access the internet from both home and internet cafes (Herold and Marolt 2011: 2–3).

China's banning of global social networking sites like Facebook, YouTube, and Twitter and the denial of access to many foreign websites have resulted in the rapid growth of Chinese firms which are offering similar services. While the government may be busy monitoring and censoring websites, ordinary Chinese users of the internet (the netizens) and smartphones use both legal and illegal ways to circumvent government restrictions and connect with one another within and outside of China (Zheng 2008; Yang 2009). Lu and Qiu (2013) argue that the increased use of the internet, especially microblogging, has the potential to foment social change in China. Chinese microblogs manifest certain crucial features that allow them to exert widespread social influences, such as the ability to mobilise people and coordinate social activities; encourage opposition to authority; organise campaigns such as charitable activities; enable the emergence of opinion leaders with groups of enthusiastic followers, and cause the unleashing of internet mobs and violence.

Most existing research on the internet and social media in China focuses on government regulation and censorship, popular culture, and state–society relations (e.g. Tai 2006; Sun 2011; Yang 2015; Negro 2017; Han 2018). In recent years, there has been increasing scholarly attention on religion and media in mainland China, Taiwan, and Hong Kong. The volume of essays (Travagnin 2017) on this subject is a good representation of a small but growing body of work. In this chapter, we want to contribute to existing research on religion and media in the Chinese context by examining how mobile internet and social media can facilitate the formation of online religious communities (cf. Ho 2017; Huang 2017). The Chinese Christians who are residing in China make overwhelming use of local mobile social media apps like WeChat, Weibo, and QQ, since most of them are unable to use foreign social media like Facebook and Twitter. However, Chinese Christians residing abroad who wish to establish and connect with religious networks in China often use a range of Chinese and foreign social media tools. For example, they may use Facebook and WhatsApp when communicating with friends and fellow Christians overseas, and switch to WeChat and Weibo when communicating with people in China. Realising the internet's potential for enabling believers to form online communities, organise religious activities, spread religious messages, and mobilise believers to engage in Christian activities, the Chinese government has recently moved to further curtail religious activities online. Subsequently, the State Administration for Religious Affairs issued new rules on religious activities that ban live streaming of religious ceremonies on the internet, forbade criticism of the Communist Party and the country's religious policy, and disallowed religious organisations to distribute religious material or convert anyone. In this chapter, we examine how Chinese Christian users of social media utilise the platform to practise their religion in their everyday life and, in the process, spread Christian values with the aim of changing the society at large. We refer to this process as the networked transmission of religious values.

The chapter is organised as follows: first, we briefly discuss the development of mobile social media in the context of China and highlight how its increasing popularity among ordinary Chinese people lends itself to the conceptualisation of Chinese popular culture. Given its ubiquity, Chinese Christians are also using social media (especially mobile chat apps) for religious communication, such as sharing of Bible passages and videos with Christian content; personal reflections on religious and social events, prayers, and pastoral care. Second, we explore the Christian concept of fellowship as the key to understanding the formation of Christian communities via social media. Subsequently, we discuss how the two processes of media mixing and intercontextuality on social media interactions facilitate the embedding of religious values into Christian users' daily lives. In this sense, the formation of online Christian communities is also about the practice of everyday religion. Finally, we discuss some limitations of the use of social media for building fellowship, particularly with reference to China's political environment and regulatory regime on internet and social media usage.

Christianity online

A recent body of scholarship on interactions between technology and society has focused on technology as embodiment and subjectivity in relation to our environment. In this sense, technology is integral to the human application of knowledge that connects people inter-subjectively with one another and the material world. In this process, people come to shape their ideas of who they are and mould the constitutions of their society and culture (Ellul 1964; Castells 2001). A similar line of reflection has emerged in the scholarship of media and religion (Lim 2009b; Campbell 2010; Lundby 2013) which examines people's construction of meaningful identities as they interact with mediated religious texts which are produced and circulated via myriad systems of communication. Some scholars have argued that the influence of the media has come to encompass social life in unprecedented degrees such that even the realm of religion can be considered thoroughly "mediatised". In other words, contemporary manifestations of religiosity in its social, cultural, and political dimensions are integrally shaped by the logics of media (Hjarvard 2008, 2011). In a highly industrialised, media-saturated society, media may act as both the producers and distributors of religious symbols and practices. The mediatisation of religion manifests several features about social media. First, social media serve as the primary source of information about religious issues. This also means that the media has the huge potential to define and frame religious issues. Second, religious information and experiences are moulded according to the demands of popular media genres. Third, media institutions are gradually taking over many of the social functions that used to be performed by religious institutions, such as societal rituals, moral orientation, and community formation.

Some years ago, Helland (2005) proposed a widely discussed distinction between "religion online" and "online religion". The former refers to information about religion that is accessible via computer-mediated networks. In China, many both official and unofficial Christian organisations have their own websites which carry information about their activities and various aspects of the Christian faith, such as key beliefs, history, evangelism, and links with other Christian groups outside China. Such examples include ccctspm.org (中国基督教网站), chinacatholic.org (信德网), and gospeltimes.cn (福音时报). Gospeltimes.cn allows readers to share its articles and videos via 56 social networking sites. Some independent churches even have their own regular online publications (e.g. *Aiyan*, *Xinghua*). On the other hand, "online religion" refers to the various ways in which religious faith is practised over these networks. Nowadays, this distinction is increasingly breaking down as most websites offer believers both information and opportunities to practise their faith, such as sharing Bible passages and prayers in the forums; watching video streams of sermons; engaging in debates over theological or pastoral matters, and plugging into translocal and transnational networks of Christian communities via hyperlinks. The hugely popular video sharing site Youku has many videos and programs with Christian themes, such as the *Daily Song* (每日一歌), which form an integral part of a Christian spiritual cultivation. The interactivity that the internet affords its users can facilitate the formation of online religious communities where members share information, hold debates, provide mutual support, plan activities, etc. (Brasher 2001; Campbell 2005; Han and Kamaludeen 2016). In an interview with the online *Christian Times*, a Protestant preacher from a church in Guangzhou province noted that:

> In this Information Age, whoever seizes the opportunities of the internet shall have the right to speak. Whether you like it or not, or whether you are used to it, you will have to adapt, as the internet is the language of this generation! The utilization of this means of communication is the challenge we face in spreading the Gospel and in building the Church; it is also the path that we need to take [our translation].

Given that the internet is a form of communication media, it can facilitate a sense of togetherness among Christians through the formation of an online religious community. Campbell's (2005) characterisation of the internet as a "sacramental space" primarily adopts an instrumental approach in the understanding of various religious groups' use of the internet, in the sense that the cyberspace is used mainly as "a space for personal spiritual pursuits and a social spiritual support sphere". In recent years, the explosion in new media technologies like internet-enabled social networking sites, such as Facebook, Twitter, Instagram, Weibo, and WeChat, has caused seismic shifts in the ways people conduct their social activities, which include religious practices. With social media, Christian groups can facilitate their group activities, form networks with the international Christian community, and share diverse views about their Christian beliefs.

To understand why many Chinese Christians create online communities on the internet and mobile, it is necessary to understand their motivation from a Christian perspective. Theologically, the community of the faithful (or ***koinonia***) is a fundamental value of Christian identity (Lohfink 1984). For Christians, salvation "is the work of God in creating *covenant community*" (Kraus 1993: 32, italics added). From this perspective of community and salvation, Jesus is seen calling his followers out of the "old Israel" into the "new Israel", which refers to a new community of believers (ibid.). The Body of Christ, namely, the Church, fundamentally comprises a community of believers. Originating from the traditional biblical sense, the expression "a community of Christians" refers to the physical gathering of fellow believers, often in their homes and temples of worship. In such "covenant communities", the believers discuss their understanding of scriptures, share meals together, as well as celebrate rituals like the Passover. In this biblical sense, Christians gather to share about their lives and provide mutual support to sustain their faith.

Paul was a leader of a prayer group that comprised software engineers working in an engineering firm in Shenzhen. He was studying theology in Singapore at the time of our interview. For him, social media has enabled him and other Christians in China to receive and watch videos of sermons conducted by preachers in Indonesia. These sermons were particularly popular with university students in China and shared widely in campuses. Another informant, Wen, was a woman in her early 20s who was working in a factory in Singapore at the time of our interview. Her experience typifies the kind of Chinese Christian transnational connectivity that has been made possible by the global reach of mobile internet and social media. Here, she shared her baptism experience:

> I posted the pictures of my baptism on QQ, and everyone was able to view it, as I did not set any restrictions to it. Many of my classmates asked me, "What are you doing?", because there was a certificate to show for it. I told them that I had been baptised. Then they asked me why do I need to be baptised? What is baptism? I told them that it's a process for becoming a Christian. They then asked me why I believe in Christianity; you are a Chinese and you still believe in it? Two days after I saw the comment, I told them that whatever it is, this is my choice and they must respect that. After that my friend explained to me that she said that because she hoped that I can bring her into Christianity as well.

Thus, for many Christians, a community forged on social media allows fellow believers to account to one another and strengthen one another's faith, so that they are less likely to fall into sin and be distracted from the path of faith. In the context of contemporary China, scholars of religion have noted that the decline of public morality in society has motivated many Chinese to turn to religion, including Christianity, to seek out new foundations of morality (e.g. Zhuo 2000; Kuah-Pearce 2014; Liang 2014; Weller and Wu 2017). Consequently, Chinese Christian communities become even more socially significant for its members as it is the trusted space in which they could cultivate morality through the practice of fellowship. On this issue, Wen has this to say:

> Every time I visit the church group, I will only see content that has been posted by the church people, I think it's alright as we are all from the same religion. We view the same things and discuss the same issues. However, when I return to my own newsfeed, there are many different activities there. Some of my friends are Buddhists, and there was once a friend asked me if there are any benefits after believing in Christ, has anything happened, etc.? I told her that at least I am not doing any bad deed and I know what I am doing is good although others might not know about it.

As social media usage has become an integral part of Chinese Christians' daily activities, and as these believers begin to use the communication tool for religious purposes, religion is less likely to be regarded by the believers as constituting a distinct domain which is separate from their ordinary, mundane experiences. This is illustrated in the comments of a Chinese Christian who was a member of a Bible study group in Singapore:

> Since we are constantly online on Facebook, we can check it the moment we are on our phones. I have also added a group from church on Facebook, and there are people who post content there every day. If they feel that a certain song is nice and suggest that this song can bring consolation or praise to

> others, they will post it directly there and share it with others to listen. I can view on my mobile phone every day on what others have posted, and click into the link to view the contents.

The religious leaders we interviewed acknowledged that the rising popularity of the internet and social networking sites is a trend that they could not ignore and has significantly impacted their work. Due to the rapid pace of communications on social media, religious leaders often must decide what messages they should respond to, and how they should intervene in online conversations. When asked if he was expected to immediately reply to someone who has posted a problem or question for him, a Protestant pastor said:

> I am sure that they do anticipate our replies, as such I definitely feel that ever since the rise of the internet, we got busier. For example, there can be up to a hundred messages waiting for your response in just one morning, you have to spend some time to look at them slowly. Sometimes I don't constantly look at WhatsApp, as I am too busy. But I am sure that they do hope to get replies from us.

As many Christians, especially the younger ones, were using social media for much of their everyday communications, religious leaders sometimes felt overwhelmed by the demand for their attention on social media. Some became highly selective and cautious in their usage of social media, especially pertaining to the veracity on the vast amount of information circulated online. Pastor Yeung, who was based in Hong Kong, said that he would respond promptly only to pastoral care matters, and refrain from re-posting unverified and unverifiable information:

> When someone is sick, or has met an accident, and when people share prayers, I will respond immediately. Otherwise, I seldom respond. Especially, for example, on Facebook, blogs or some websites, because I think there is too many information. Some information is shared from their friends, from the internet, they will immediately share. But they don't have the time to check if it's true or not. Often, people don't have the judgment or have time to think about the information being shared but they circulate it.

Media mixing and intercontextuality

We argue in this chapter that the activities of religious actors (both individually and in groups) conducted via social media and mobile internet cause them to further embed "religion" into their everyday social life. For the rest of this chapter, we identify and analyse two main processes in which this may be achieved, namely, media mixing and intercontextuality. In the context of this chapter, the Chinese Christians' mixing of media types refers to their online sharing, embedding, and mutual referencing of various religious media files such as religious texts, pictures, videos, and audio recordings. This process may facilitate the integration of religious practices and rituals in the daily lives of Chinese Christians in different geographical locations, thus creating fellowship as they access and use social media for everyday communication needs. One of our interviewees, Susan, who worked as an IT specialist in Shenzhen at the time of our interview, attributed the immense popularity and appeal of mobile social media apps like WeChat to how they provide greater ease for users to express their feelings and emotions:

> Our office has created a group, too. Yes, it's the few of us Christians. We *often socialise* online in that group ...The main thing about Weixin is that it is *convenient.* It has appealed to a weakness in men: men don't like to type! Weixin has a *voice* function for communication...We can have a full video chat. And with WIFI, we can see each other face to face to chat. It's the video that I feel have successfully overcome many men's weakness, their laziness. And for women to express their feelings. For example, they can naturally post any feelings, with *pictures* and even *videos* [emphasis added].

By posting and mutually referencing different media files on social media, Chinese Christians in China and elsewhere are able to create, disseminate, and interpret religious content. They are also able to encourage those who have received these media files to engage in religious practices in their daily lives. At the same time, they become participants in mutual encouragement and monitoring. Believers could access these media files and choose to respond to them at convenient times such as when they are commuting, at home, waiting for trains, and in a queue. In the process, they are establishing, maintaining, and consolidating religious networks. These networks link Chinese Christians in different localities. In our interview, May, a young woman from China working in a factory in Singapore, shared with us how she was able to participate in online religious rituals and activities by accessing and interacting with multiple media files on Facebook. These were uploaded by her church members when she was unable to attend services:

> Because in the society now, it is really difficult to meet up and pray together, it is not practical. If we write on Facebook, everyone can pray together after reading the content. It wouldn't be like, if during a certain month I am unable to attend service because of some matters, then I wouldn't be able to share my thoughts with them face-to-face and discuss the matter together. If we post it on Facebook, everyone can give you opinions and advice in the commentary area, and you yourself will be able to view it. There, people can view it anytime and check the latest updates. I think this is better.

Therefore, the mixing of different media types in social media communications enables religious practices, such as prayers, Bible sharing, mediation, preaching, and worship, to become more integrated into the daily lives and settings of the believers. These practices are no longer confined to the specifically demarcated "religious" space such as a physical church building at delineated "religious" services times. Jacob, an IT professional based in Singapore, articulates:

> I think that gospel is not a specific scenario which is only limited to the churches. Gospel should be the everyday life, a world-view, and it is affecting

> your every move, it also gets further reflections from your every action. So, I can talk about playing basketball with you, and I can also talk about songs with you. Moreover, all of them can reflect some of the basic qualities in our beliefs, which can help us to reflect on. Do our faiths exist only in churches, a fixed location, on Sunday?

Another way Chinese Christians create transnational fellowship on social media is through intercontextuality. In interactional sociolinguistics, intercontextuality refers to "the social construction of relationships among events and contexts" (Bloome et al. 2009: 319). In practice, intercontextuality involves the social media user's efforts at connecting a set of events happening in different times and places. This connecting of events in turn needs to be recognised by others on the same social network as meaningful and consequential from a religious perspective. For example, following the deadly Ya'an earthquake in Sichuan province in April 2013 that killed around 200 people, Christian netizens flooded Weibo, the Chinese Twitter equivalent, with posts to express their views and interpretations of the disaster, mainly from a Christian perspective. One post quoted the passage from Revelation 16:15 ("See, I am coming like a thief! Blessed is the one who stays awake and is clothed, not going about naked and exposed to shame") to exhort the readers to be "awake [as] the time of our Lord's return is near!" (*China Church Voices*).

In another example, the Facebook post below (Figure 3.1) shows how a believer wished to integrate prayers into her attempts at learning origami:

Figure 3.1 Intercontextuality: learning origami as a form of prayer.

In the post above, the user talked about her prayer, sleep, and origami, all in one post. From this, we can see how prayer was integrated into her daily activities (such as sleep and handicraft) and formed an important part of her identity as a Christian. Such posts often elicit messages of encouragement and affirmation from fellow Christians. Her engagement in prayer, in the midst of mundane activities, also imbued these activities with a deeper spiritual meaning. As this example illustrates, intercontextuality in social media allows the communication of religious practices like prayer, reflection, and worship singing to take place in the same space as Chinese Christians' daily activities such as cooking, eating, studying, going on retreats, and moving house.

The mobile app WeChat hosts numerous Christianity-related services, activities, and products which are available to mobile phone users. One such service provider is the Christian Psychological Services (心理咨询基督教服务处). We were alerted to this mobile service by Debby, a young Christian who was an avid user of mobile apps, including the one in which she consulted for articles and advice on issues related to marriage life. Debby told us,

> The way I got to know about this service is a good example of how social media sites mediate relationships and transmit information: one of my acquaintances on WeChat subscribed to its updates, which could be seen in her personal WeChat page viewed on my own mobile phone.

The service provider's introduction on WeChat stated: "We are a group of Christians. Among us there are government-registered psychotherapists, highly experienced counsellors, and pastors and preachers". Its main service was to answer queries on "marital, family and psychological matters" and to "foster a full and happy life". While much of the daily updates focused on these matters, there was also much sharing of Bible reflections, links to articles on personal issues written from a Christian perspective; announcements on religious events and daily Bible quizzes, etc. Thus, this app on WeChat functions as an intercontextual process that allows religion, commerce, psychotherapy, family life, and personal consumption to converge and interact with one another as an integrated experience for the users. Through such intercontextuality, Christian values are potentially transmitted across these different social domains.

We also observed another WeChat group which comprises members who are Chinese Christian professionals who attended the same church in Shanghai. They were part of a Bible study group that was led by a Chinese Christian who had studied and worked in Singapore for about eight years. This leader, Cynthia, worked in a city in China. The WeChat group consisted of ten members of her Bible study group; a Singaporean couple who were from the church she attended in Singapore; another Singaporean couple from the same Singaporean church but who were based in Singapore; and a Singaporean teacher. Most of the conversation revolved around the adaptation problems that Cynthia experienced in moving from working in Singapore to China. It started with her complaints about her work situation in China and her struggles with the complex relationships at work. She shared that her colleagues were either gossiping about one another or conniving to remove one another from the company. She was in a dilemma since she knew that as a Christian she should not be involved in such activities. This situation finally ended when she was asked to leave the company. However, this was the beginning of another set of struggles in which she wavered between looking a job in China, going to the United States for theological education, and purchasing public housing apartment in Singapore. The long conversation in WeChat centred around her dilemma and struggles in her decisions.

Her Christian friends, consisting of both the Chinese Christians in her Bible study group in China and the Singaporean couple in Singapore, offered advice based on the Bible and their evaluation of her situation. Pauline, her friend from her Bible study group in China, encouraged her by quoting verses from the Bible, and urged her to find a prayer partner who could meet her to pray regularly, so that she could receive the social support that she needed. The Singaporean couple was concerned that Cynthia might be seeking to escape from her difficult situation in China by opting to go to the United States for theological education. They were also concerned that if she went to the United States, she might just be acquiring a lot of classroom knowledge of theology which she might not know how to apply to her professional work and church when she returned to China. She replied that she was cognisant of the fact that she needed an understanding of psychology and history, apart from theology, to understand the social problems and needs in China. The example of Cynthia's thus further illustrates how the practice of intercontextuality on social media enables the weaving of spiritual matters and meditation in Chinese Christians' daily lives. Such intercontextual form of communication on social media also creates a feeling of "openness" among members and conveys the message that they could offer support to one another. This, in turn, fosters a sense of community and solidarity among group members.

Intercontextuality in the social media may also enable Christian users to connect seemingly non-religious and religious topics, in accordance with their judgement of appropriateness and suitability. Elaine, from Wenzhou, shared Christian material in the social media so that others might read and understand more about Christianity:

> The Weixin platform was handled by me previously, the basic source of information that I get was from the people I know and the preachers, as well as the spiritual journals that they wrote, and I would put these information on Weixin. I would update every day, and also, as there are non-believers in our followers and audience, we would also input information regarding things like *solutions to solve family or work problems* [emphasis].

In sum, media mixing and intercontextuality on social media enable Chinese Christian users to discursively and practically meld religious matters and with other daily activities. The everyday Christianity that we seek to describe here is facilitated by the widespread use of social media as a form of popular culture.

Shepherding the flock: pastoral care

The rapid adoption of mobile social media by the Chinese society at large has also exerted a profound impact on how the clergy perform their work, especially in pastoral care. Before the era of smartphones and Web 2.0, much of the clergy's pastoral work had to be done via face-to-face encounters. In the contemporary times, the Chinese Christian clergy are embracing the opportunities offered by the internet and social networking sites increasingly to extend their pastoral work in the daily lives of the members. No longer are they confined to the physical churches or other venues where religious activities take place. Their increasing online presence, made possible via computers and smartphones, means that the believers can contact one other more easily. In addition, they can potentially reach and influence their followers in a more immediate way via social networking apps which are downloaded into smartphones. These smartphones follow the owners wherever they are, resulting in the formation of Christian "portable communities" (Chayko 2008). In one of our interviews, a Protestant clergy confided in us how important social networking sites are for his work in pastoral care:

> I feel that it aids in my pastoral work. For example, sermons are considered as a group pastoral but when it is on the internet, it becomes an individual relation. I will be able to get to know them on a deeper level individually. If they enjoy talking to you, you will have a lot of chance to get to know them. However, in the church itself, it is me, one person to many of them. I feel that the usage of internet and social media can aid in caring for the members and they work hand-in-hand with pastoral work.

Protestant Pastor Leung, who was involved in pastoral care in a Christian primary school in Hong Kong at the time of our interview, was very much aware of the advantages of the internet and social media as a communications tool for his work. For instance, he once visited an exhibition on the Mississippi river and realised he could draw his congregation's attention to the biblical significance of some of the exhibition material:

> After I visited the exhibition, I shared with my students on the internet and the link between it and the Bible. It is an interactive experience as they can reply to what I have posted and add pictures to indicate which part of the Bible it was referring to. All these are conducted on the internet. At many instances, the data that we require for our research is available on the internet; we will bookmark it and refer to it again when needed. This information comes from both the government and Christian organizations and is very useful when it comes to preaching.

Another of our interviewees, Father Andrew, a Yunnanese Catholic priest from the official Catholic Patriotic Church, was an active user of WeChat and QQ. He used these social media apps to communicate with fellow Christians, parishioners, and other acquaintances. In our interview, he explained how the new media technology impacted his pastoral work:

> Regarding Weixin or QQ, there is another use, and that is for others to contact me over spiritual cultivation matters. In this situation, I can give some help, and the outcomes are usually good. That's because this person knows me, knows I'm able to help resolve his problems, and is looking for someone to talk to.

Each day, our respondent, Father Andrew, would post a couple of his Bible reflections on WeChat. Many of these posts would elicit responses and stimulate further discussions. In response to a post on 26 February 2014, an acquaintance wrote, "I often follow Father's reflections, a few words will provide clear guidance to a troubled soul". To this, Father Andrew replied: "Thanks for your encouragement. Let's journey together in God's Kingdom". In addition, the priest also conducted catechism via WeChat by uploading excerpts from the Catechism of the Catholic Church on his page as can be seen in Figure 3.2.

Figure 3.2 Pastoral care on social media. Left: Reflections on Bible passages. Right: Teaching of catechism.

The screenshot in Figure 3.3 was taken from another Catholic priest's WeChat page, showing the titles and topics of the posts, and examples of Christian advice and activities like "Let go of others' wrongdoing and liberate your heart", "2017 Summer Camp: get to know the living God, enjoy the holidays together", and "San Mao's [a late popular author] 20 most poignant quotes". The post on 13 June is about how one can get to know a person's character through their attitude towards money.

Let go of others' wrongdoing and liberate your heart.

When one borrows money, you can see one's heart; when one returns money, you can see one's character.

2017 Summer Camp: get to know the living God, enjoy the holidays together

Tears flow uncontrollably upon rereading San Mao's [a late popular author] 20 most poignant quotes.

Do not let prayers become "accessories"! God will lovingly accept this kind of prayers ...

Figure 3.3 Priest's postings on society and morality.

Limitations of social media in nurturing *koinonia*

As we have seen from the discussion above, media mixing and intercontextuality in social media facilitate the discussion of spiritual matters and encourage Chinese Christians to practise religion in their daily lives. At the same time, we also need to be aware of technology's limitations for the Christians in their efforts to establish transnational Chinese Christian fellowship. One of the limitations of social media which are highlighted by some of our informants concerns its potentially individualising effects. One of these social media's perceived dangers consists of the risks that Christians may engage in religious activities as individuals while avoiding face-to-face community interactions. The communications platform can also become massive distractions for Christians. For Pastor Leung, the heightened emotional state that is generated by Christians gathering at the same time and physical space to engage in common activities is an essential element of fellowship:

> If we do our prayers alone using the internet, we will not reap from the church. Liberation is what we get from churches, and then we share it with others and encourage one another based on the teachings and our own experience and actions ... Thus, I do not agree on worshipping over the internet, unless the person is ill or overseas. People must *gather together to feel the emotions and atmosphere of the group*. There are some people who might be lying down on their bed and worship through their iPad ... Overdoing it will cause us to lose our main intentions of using these social media, which is to spread God's teaching and not spend time looking at all these social media [emphasis added].

The importance of face-to-face communication was also acknowledged by another Hong Kong–based clergy, Pastor Tse, whom we interviewed. He stressed that Christian pastoral work cannot be adequately carried out via the internet and social media apps and required the "personal touch" of face-to-face communication. He felt that this was equivalent to following in the footsteps of Jesus:

> I believe in face-to-face communication, I believe in personal touch by their own voices. That means I use my phone to comfort or to give a prayer to each other, to my friends, to my brothers and sisters. But *not through the words in the computer*...Just like for this interview, you need to get a flight from your country to come here for face-to-face interview. So as a pastor to all the Christians all over the world, it's the same thing, we need to help the sick, help the poor face-to-face. Have the physical touch. That means you can't use the telephone or the Facebook or the iPhone to go to the hospital to give a sick person to have physical appearance, to have a prayer, to have a touch, to comfort their sorrow...*just like Jesus* in the gospel. He walks by his own legs, so I think as a pastor, I think we need to follow the steps of Jesus. That means we can do the work by our own hands, our own feet [emphasis added].

Leaders: circumscribing discourses

The members of an online community often assume roles which reflect their real-life roles in the group. Leadership roles entail both spiritual and social guidance. The group leader provides the spiritual leadership through social media by encouraging the members to apply religious and spiritual capital in their daily lives and work. Formal or informal leaders play a crucial role in shaping online discourses. They intervene on matters such as appropriateness of topics and discussions, religious orthodoxy, sharing of authoritative interpretations on biblical passages, as well as censuring of those who are perceived to have transgressed notions of propriety. Our interviewee, Beth, from a rural unofficial church in Wenzhou, confessed how the leaders' online authority is based on their seniority and perceived "experience" (有经验). She also elaborated on how they may assert their influence "behind the scene" to intervene in "unusual activity":

> Some of these leaders will only monitor behind the scene. But when there is any unusual activity, there will be someone that will stand out and correct it. Although there is not much activity in the group, but we do still have a *strong sense of responsibility* within the group … We also found some suspicious people within the group and had him remove. I remembered there was once I was in a group when someone posted some heterodoxy content to advertise about some websites. The person might be confused over what is right and wrong and shared such a content with the group. Thereafter, a few of us discovered that there is something not right and we contacted the administrator to check on the person's background. We must understand that we all belong to the same church. In the end we checked with the principal the real identity of this person and had him kicked out of the group. *We do not allow such bad content in the group.*

Another of our interviewees, a leader of a young adult's group on Facebook, encouraged the members to join a spiritual seminar and pray. In addition, we observed that the social relationship established in the online faith community is transferred to the face-to-face community. This could be seen in his efforts to organise gatherings for group members. In one post, the leader of the group asked how the members were doing in the week. He proceeded to encourage them to pray and join him and the assistant leader to pray in the park. The group leader also attempted to set an example for his members, by helping the members keep in pace with the direction and vision of church. The roles played by various members of the online religious community were vital for maintenance and sustenance of their faith. In addition, the roles played by the assistant leader and informal leader were important in supporting the work of the leader, especially in terms of influencing the members from within.

It is clear from the online discourses we have access to that the formal leader of the group provided the spiritual guidance, and his assistant leader, the social and rapport building. They played similar roles in and outside the context of social media: the leader provided the spiritual guidance, and the assistant leader organised the social events. At the same time, a crossing of boundaries was observed in the social media conversation. The leader performed a regulatory role in giving instructions to members to observe some kind of order in allocation of tasks for an outdoor activity for the group, and not intervene in the ordering of groups for this task allocation. At the same time, the leader tried to maintain rapport and contact with members during the week. He expressed concern about how they were doing in their daily lives. Social media allowed him to do that when he was not able to see them face-to-face. The leader also joined in friendly exchanges with the members on every day and social matters. Concurrently, another member also provided an informal spiritual leadership by sharing spiritual texts and songs in social media.

First, this crossing of boundary was evidenced in the maintenance of the different types of leadership. In the Facebook posts of the Bible study group of Chinese Christians, we observed that there was leadership provided informally by some women in the group who mentored the other women who were "younger" in their faith. Second, the members crossed the secular-sacred boundaries by making use of the advantages of intercontextuality that social media offer. They do so to show that, first, the leaders were also the members' friends, and second, that religious activities, like prayer and Bible study, could take place in a social setting. This point is obviously a very important attraction to the mainland Chinese who valued the social aspects of church life very highly. They looked for the social support and mentorship. Third, in social media, the leader and members were able to find out the happenings at various levels of the group's involvements. Such crossing of boundaries allows for the integration of the various expressions of self in an act of worship: social; private, and public activities; entertainment; work, as well as religious and secular practices. In addition, this transcendence of boundaries results in the formation of the social-sacred, which enables the believers to apply their faith in different dimensions of their lives. It also enables them to communicate and practise their faith in their daily lives in a way that transcends the restrictions which are placed by the state. In the online Christian communities, the leaders and members play different roles in constructing the religious and spiritual capital of the group. This reinforces a sense of solidarity in the group in the sense that they are all participating in different functions to bring the group together.

Pastor Chan, who was from Hong Kong, said he viewed certain political discussions on Christian social media as "inappropriate" and, hence, would refrain from participating or responding to these discussions as a way of discouraging such activities:

> For example, there is a youngster who loves to talk about politics in the WhatsApp group. I will only look at those messages but not reply directly to them, as it is not very appropriate. It is not that I do not reply them, but I choose to reply them *in private* because if I reply them openly on the web, everyone is able to view them, and I do not want others to interpret my comments in a wrong way as it will be very difficult for me to explain myself thereafter. I seldom discuss about political matters on the web, I only talk about them at home as we do not know if anyone will quote your words and spread to others. I will also be more cautious when discussing religious matter on social media with Christians in Mainland China because we cannot tell if they are able to bypass the security. I am not afraid as I am in Hong Kong; I am more worried for my counterparts in mainland China.

Thus, Pastor Chan's position was that political discussions should be held in private, and not in the more public domain of social media, especially when interacting with Christians in the mainland. As someone with legitimate authority in his circle of fellow Christians, he was able to shape the patterns of interactions and content in his social media groupings by his choice of participation in the content of discussion in social media.

"Bird-cage religion"

Since the early adoption of internet and rise of social media, China has witnessed internet activism and critical voices on social media (e.g. Zheng 2008; Yang 2009; Lu and Qiu 2013; Vala and Huang 2017). The internet plays a critical role in collective action and allows social forces to react in a rapid and efficient way. For example, the internet allows for a new way of organising protests (Liu 2006). It becomes a way for the Chinese people to harness a bottom-up force to counteract the top-down propaganda of the regime (Liu 2006). Whether the Chinese people succeed to achieve their aims in their collective actions or face a crackdown by the government depends on whether the government sees it to be a threat to their legitimacy or constructive actions for the state (Zheng 2008). However, even the attempts of the government to control this online social action are met with protests by the large population of Chinese internet users (Yang 2009). Many protests that have erupted in recent years have been mobilised via online media. In their analysis of the microblogging activities of three prominent Protestant personalities in Weibo, Vala and Huang (2017) argue that these bloggers have been exposing Protestant Christianity to a wide Chinese audience and enhancing deeper understanding of the faith among existing Christians, while at times seeking to challenge the party-state's discourse on religious affairs. Lu and Qiu (2013) identify opposition to the authorities as one of the features of Chinese social media like Weibo microblog. This is primarily because the Chinese state dominates many aspects of social life in the country. In contrast, in our research, our Chinese Christian informants eschewed criticising the Chinese government openly on social media. One important reason was that they did not wish to draw undue government attention to their Christian communities and negatively affect their social media acquaintances. We have discussed previously how in Christian social media groups, users may shift between explicitly talking about "religious" and "non-religious" issues; for example, they can converse about arranging meeting for social activities, gossiping about friends, commenting on current affairs, etc. in the same post. However, the Chinese Christian users we spoke with treated one domain of conversation with great caution, namely, politics. The current Chinese political leadership under the "core leader" Xi Jinping regards online criticism and mobilisation as posing a severe threat to its authority. It has unleashed a wide-ranging and intensive crackdown on the internet and social media usage with the use of draconian regulations, intensive surveillance and censorship, shutting down of blogs, jailing dissidents and bloggers, and even banning of certain words such as "civil society". In all our interviews conducted with mainland Chinese Christians, it is very evident that they were highly cautious about the kinds of information they communicated on social media. As Marolt (2011: 60–61) notes, Chinese users of the internet

> are not interested in contesting the control of the Chinese state over Chinese society, but rather in ***avoiding*** and ***bypassing*** the surveillance and control mechanisms of the state in their own ***everyday*** lives, thus ***dodging unwanted influences on their thoughts, practices, and actions*** [italics added].

Despite the government's intense surveillance and control of the internet in China, Chinese Christians, particularly those from the house churches, are still able to connect with discourses of the global Christian community through their online communications. The transnational networks enable the international Christian community to form solidarity in fellowship with the Chinese Christians who may be facing challenging circumstances such as official censorship and demolition of churches in Wenzhou. Figure 3.4 is a post on WeChat on the demolition of churches by the Zhejiang government, which highlights the solidarity in fellowship which is enabled by social media of Chinese Christians in the face of government crackdown. This can be accessed, read, commented upon, and further circulated by Chinese Christians in and outside of the country who use the mobile app.

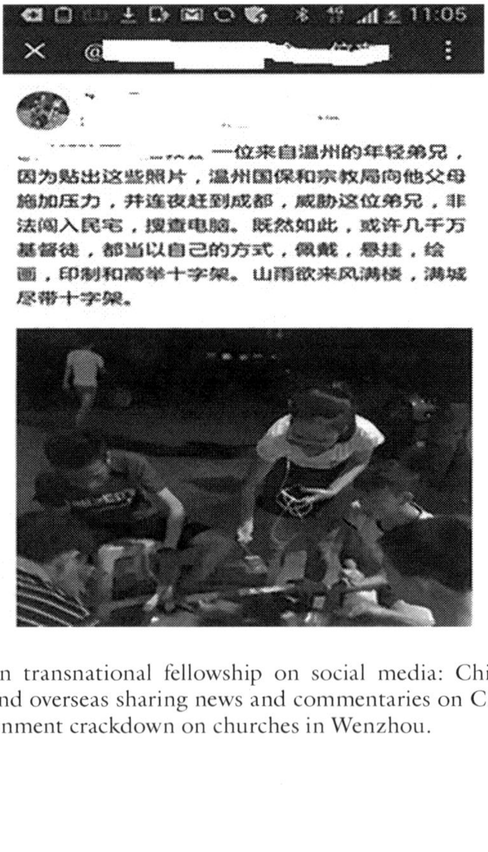

Figure 3.4 Christian transnational fellowship on social media: Chinese Christians in China and overseas sharing news and commentaries on Christians' responses to government crackdown on churches in Wenzhou.

The example of the Facebook post, as shown in Figure 3.4 above, is an illustration of how Christian fellowship can be created using social media, bringing together Christians within and outside China to focus on a common cause and foster Christian fellowship. Through the local and global connections forged via digital networks—even with strong government internet control—the concerns and issues in China such as poverty, official corruption, social injustice, environmental pollution, and political tensions can become shared concerns among Christians from China and elsewhere. The converse is true too: Chinese Christians residing in the country are able to engage with global events. Thus, conceptually and practically, intercontextuality on social media allows Chinese Christian users to fuse the local and global, the secular and religious, and the mundane and transcendental.

With the intense state monitoring of online activities in China, Chinese Christians we spoke with often expressed reservations about sharing personal and religious matters using social media. One of our interviewees, Qian Yu, who was from an independent church in a rural part of Wenzhou, had personally experienced the effects of state surveillance. She expressed how it had instilled fear among her and her fellow undergraduates who belonged to an independent church:

> Yes, I do have reservations, so do many people around me. People around my age usually have certain level of reservation. This is related to life experience. If you've ever been monitored or stopped from doing something, everyone will know immediately...When I was in university, there were organisations which were not openly known. During that time, churches had already been keeping a low profile. The government allowed them to exist, but they could act any time to stop you from conducting any activities. They might even arrest you. The situation improved after graduation as we were no longer monitored by them. During our student days, we were still under their monitoring, we were afraid that they might prevent us graduating from university and we would not be able to answer to our parents...The internet and social media can be used by Christians to build religious communities and solidarity, and many are aware of these media's mobilising potential. But when size grows too big or publicly active, the government is likely to respond harshly.

Another of our interviewees, Jacob, who was the leader of a group of Chinese factory workers based in Singapore at the time of our interview, looked unfavourably upon overseas Chinese Christians who openly criticised the Chinese government on social media. He personally took great care to avoid discussing political issues with Christian acquaintances from the mainland. He strongly felt that, as a Christian, it would be "more effective" if he had demonstrated Christian values such as kindness in everyday life, rather than protest about public issues in social media. He felt a personal responsibility to protect Chinese Christians in China by not implicating them in discussions of controversial issues on social media. According to him, many of those who discussed religion and social issues explicitly on social media were based overseas and, hence, outside the immediate reach of the Chinese authorities:

> If someone really needs to post any sensitive remark, for example, on religion and politics, then regardless of what social network he uses, he will be under surveillance. Technically no one can escape from the censor. People who talk about religious things on Sina blog, I have a feeling that most of them are outside the country. A large part of the talk is about social reform. So, the starting point of this group of people may be political or religious, or it is political cloaked in religious garb, or religious cloaked in political garb, it is hard to say. They are either migrants or visiting scholars. In fact, some of these people may post some irresponsible remarks. He may not worry about his speeches, but his speeches are likely to pose threats to a few vulnerable domestic groups. Or it may enable the Chinese government to tighten its policy as a whole regarding religion.

Most of our informants took for granted that the state authorities, such as the Public Security, were monitoring all forms of online interactions, and, hence, would avoid discussing matters that could attract the attention of the authorities. These matters included visiting foreign Christian missionaries; preachers and speakers; Chinese politics and the Communist Party; Sino-Vatican relations; Taiwan; Tibet; Xinjiang; and human rights. Some informants mentioned visits to their church premises by officials from the local Religious Affairs Bureau and Public Security. The security personnel seemed to know beforehand that there would be foreign speakers present. Along this vein, a Protestant lay leader of an independent church in Chengdu said:

> Previously, there was a professor from America who came here for a church sharing. It was then when the police came. The police, somehow, were informed beforehand about such events. If they want to find you, it is actually a simple task for them. If they want to stop such events from happening, they can simply make use of this information available to do so.

Thus, Christian users' communication in social media both constructs and reinforces their interpersonal relationships and roles. It is also an implicit negotiation of their relations with the Chinese state. Though Chinese Christians may overtly voice their discontent and anger towards the authorities and on social injustice, they are very cautious that they are not seen as resisting the state as members of their respective Christian groups. Father Andrew, the Catholic priest from the officially organised Patriotic Church, quipped that the state authorities wanted Christianity to be a "bird-cage religion" (鸟笼式的宗教). For him and many Christians he knew, the internet and social networking sites were used primarily for "spreading the Gospel, reflections of the faith and Bible passages", and not for discussing broader social and political issues.

> I think the more "sensitive issues" today, from the perspective of religion, would probably be China-Vatican relations, this involves the appointment of the bishops, and Taiwan issue, and so on. Also, you must see who is discussing these issues. If you ask experts based in Hong Kong, this is not realistic. If you ask Ye Xiaowen [former head of the Religious Bureau], then it might not be a problem ... In this present context of pluralism, boundaries are still present ... For me, it's just about spreading the Gospel, bible reflection, faith reflection, and such matters ...To the authorities, the more you write about "bird-cage" kind of matters, the better!

Another of our interviewees, a Protestant lay leader from the independent church in Chengdu, also expressed being cautious on social media:

> I feel that certain sensitive issues should not be discussed in those kinds of channels. I guess the police have not been very strict about these social media. I feel that they think that there is no need to bother about these, but when they decide to take action, they can do so easily...Thus, when we send out messages, we tweak some of the words to make it sound more "correct". For example, if we are hold a bible writing session on Friday night, I would phrase it as "we are meeting for a learning session again", and "at the same old venue". I will only use very neutral words so that people outside the circle will not be able to decipher the message.

Li Juan, a Christian leader from Wenzhou who was studying at a Bible college in Singapore at the time of our interview, was not a keen user of social media platforms when it comes to sharing her views and feelings on religious matters. She confessed that she "was lazy" and acknowledged the usefulness of such communication tools for religious purposes. Li Juan had a friend "who shares quotes from the bible frequently" and he told him that "what he is doing is very good". She would "only appear and comment" when she felt the need to and would remain silent during the small talks and gossips on social media. Apart from self-confessed "laziness", an important reason Li Juan was not an enthusiastic user of social media was due to government surveillance, saying that "it is too dangerous" to use social media to publicise gatherings". Li Juan and her fellow Christians believed that their phones were tapped too. As a result, she knew many Christian leaders who carry multiple phones in order to circumvent government surveillance. Since many Christian groups and churches in Wenzhou, and elsewhere in China, sought to establish ties with their counterparts overseas, and vice versa, interactions with foreigners have become a "sensitive" issue. As a church leader, Li Juan was particularly mindful of the need to handle this matter well:

> Chinese government is still worried about your connections with foreigners as it might implicate political matters. I believe this is linked to the origin of the religion in China. Buddhism has already been localised as it has already

> been in China for a long time. Christianity is different, same for Islam. In the western part of China, Islam is very secretive. The situation might be better for Christianity. The government does not take strong actions towards the religion, but they continue to monitor the organisations. There are times where the monitoring is extra strict like during major events or periodic changes. During these periods, the monitoring over the internet will be more extensive, same for mobile phones. There are also times when they are more relaxed. It all depends on the political situations then. *We all understand how this works*, when something big is happening in the country, we should not be too aggressive in our actions or else the authority will hit you hard.

Hong was part of our focus group interview with a group of professionals based in Shenzhen. He emphasised that in his communications about public issues, he was careful to confine his discussion to his personal actions, such as giving up his seat to someone who needed it more when he was travelling on public transport. In other words, in terms of what was acceptable or unacceptable to communicate in social media, Chinese Christians often tried to distinguish between individual views and the collective views of the groups they belonged to. They were careful to protect their respective groups by not revealing specific details of their members, places, and times of gathering. They also refrained from making the association between their religious and political practices. There were different implications in what was communicated in social media in China, depending on whether the views were about public issues, or seen to represent either personal or the collective views of a Christian group. If it was a personal view, it might be tolerated by state authorities. However, if postings represented the collective view, respondents felt that these might be regarded by the authorities as some form of activism, hence potentially threatening to the state. Wen Ming, who was a volunteer with GMV, the foreign Christian NGO in mainland China, shared similar concerns over the use of social media:

> Right now we are pretty careful in using those social networks. Because we understand that the Chinese government is pretty concerned about evangelising people and they are monitoring most of these social networks. So we are pretty careful in using those. We don't use Weixin, Weibo or QQ, in an evangelical kind of conversations. We would try to use them to make friends, to socialise with them. I think that's all we would try to use.

Another of our interviewees, a Singaporean architect, Derrick, who had been involved in community development work in Sichuan, expressed how he and his co-workers were fully aware that social media and the internet was "not a private domain, it's a very public domain". Hence, they tried to highlight their "professionalism" as much as possible when they communicated with each other online, and often used "*coded, encrypted message* … some phrases that we use to substitute what we wanted to say".

> So, we usually do not communicate anything that discredits the government, we do not do anything that discredits the community, anything outside of those two areas, I think we can be quite free about what we say... And [co-workers] are also very careful about what they say, because they know the government monitors their conversations. Everybody knows. The security bureau will interview our workers as well as our students to try to understand what they do. And then, if we do anything wrong, they do not hesitate to call us and tell us that we should stop this, we should stop that. Sometimes we do, I mean some of our new colleagues were not familiar with it, they always step on these boundaries. And of course, we apologise.

From Derrick's response, we see further evidence of how Chinese Christians, particularly those from house churches, draw a boundary by refraining from talking about the "political" while they are conversing about religion. Furthermore, they juxtapose the sacred and secular in their conversations on social media in the way they "make friends" and "socialise" with acquaintances while they are praying, sharing Bible reflections, and promulgating Christian values. Thus, while some institutional boundaries are either unclear, transcended, or not recognised in social media practices, many Chinese Christian users also consciously or unwittingly maintain the boundary between "religion" and "politics". Even so, they still wish to disseminate Christian values and material, and interpret and make commentaries on important social affairs through the lens of Christianity. By considering social media as popular culture, they are able to do this precisely due to their practice of Christianity as everyday religion, which is facilitated through intercontextuality and media mixing in their social media usage.

From the preceding analyses, we can make several observations. First, simultaneous with its widespread adoption of the Chinese people in general, social media usage for religious purposes is increasingly more popular among Christians. This means that the boundaries that define Christian groupings take on a more fluid and shifting nature. Second, while the internet and social media are recognised by Christians as important tools for religious communication and practice, online interactions serve to complement, and do not replace, face-to-face interactions among the believers. Third, while there is ample evidence of religious symbols and discourses moving across social domains in the online environment, the domain which is still largely out of bounds is "politics". This is because of the widespread view among Chinese Christians about the ruling Communist Party's online surveillance and intolerance of dissent. Many Christian users of the internet and mobile apps who are residents in China, particularly those from house churches, assiduously avoid engaging in explicitly "political" activities and "activism". We should not infer from the practice of such precautionary measures that Chinese Christians try to separate "religion" from "politics" and refuse to be socially engaged. In fact, from our interviews, the converse is often true—religion, as everyday religion, tends to encompass different domains of social life, including the political domain. In other words, our Chinese Christians respondents' general avoidance of "politics" or "sensitive issues" on social media does not necessarily imply they are apolitical. Due to repressive state control, they could be socially engaged in less obtrusive ways, through their engagement with social media in which they embed Christian messages and values in various aspects of daily life via intercontextuality on social media.

Conclusion

In this chapter, we adopt an analytical perspective that considers online religion as everyday religion, and social media and religion, as deeply embedded in Chinese culture. As Robert and White (2007: 12) notes, "The movement away from religion as institution and dogmatic and moral propositions to religion as culture has brought much for attention to aspects of religion which are important in the everyday lives of the people". Specifically, we have identified and examined how media mixing and intercontextuality on social media have enabled Chinese Christians to integrate religious values in their everyday life in the forging of the social sacred. In what we refer to as networked transmission of religious values, social media allow our Chinese Christians respondents the space to discuss different aspects of their lives such as religious practices and activities related to daily lives and work. Informed by their religious values, they weave these different facets of their lives in their engagement with social media, as part of meaning-making process. Hence, in our observation of their social media posts, we discovered that the Chinese Christians' efforts in praying and meditations on the Bible were often interwoven with talk about their professional work, global news events, socialising, commentaries of daily happenings, and other seemingly mundane matters. In their social media posts, the communication of religious practices like prayer, preaching, and worship singing took place in the same media space as communication of members' daily activities, such as cooking, eating, studying, going on retreats, and moving to a new house. Our analysis of their posts reveals that they were motivated (but not only) by religious beliefs and principles to participate in online groups and discussion, thereby cultivating social ties which were supported by religious networks. The sought-after solidarity and strengthened sense of identity then became resources for their negotiation of moral maze in daily life.

We conclude by making two points in relation to the substantive concern of this chapter. First, Chinese Christians may use social media for "social" or "socialising" purposes. We are not asserting that all Chinese Christians or other religious believers are constantly trying to spread Christian messages when using the social media or frame all activities they conduct on these platforms in religious terms. What we are trying to analyse and highlight in this chapter is how Chinese Christians, if they wish to, may seek to imbue their social media communications with religious significance and in turn spread religious values through their online networks. In doing so, they may circumvent the restrictions imposed by the authorities. In addition, due to the widespread use of the media as popular culture, they may allude to Christian values and viewpoints without being explicitly evangelistic. The media mixing and intercontextuality on social media platforms thus enable Chinese Christian users to communicate about their daily routines and Christian values on a regular basis. At the individual level, this fusing of religion with daily activities often blurs or ignores the institutional distinction between the "religious" and "non-religious". Commenting on online religion as lived religion, Helland (2005) notes:

> In the case of online religion, people are living their religion on and through the internet medium. For those individuals who participate in online religious activity, there is no separation between their offline life and experiences and their online life and experiences, and their religious activities and worldview permeate both environments.

Many of our respondents seek to practise Christian values in their everyday life, in strong contrast with, and in response to, the perceived decline of morality in China. As they try to spread Christian values and messages to their online non-Christian acquaintances (such as at the workplace), they are also engaging in a form of social engagement, albeit in a non-obtrusive manner. By this, we refer to how they regard Christian values as possible solutions to many social and moral problems in China. While doing so, they may also seek to align their Christian concerns with wider societal issues. Building that online fellowship was important to them and it also affirmed their Christian conscience about the state of morality or lack of it in the society at large. They may be motivated by religious beliefs and principles to participate in online groups and discussion. The sought-after solidarity and strengthened sense of identity through social media communications then become spiritual resources for their negotiation of moral maze in daily life.

Second, on social media our Chinese Christian respondents tend to draw boundaries around the two domains of their online conversation, namely, the "religious" and the "political" as institutionally defined in China, in order to avoid run-ins with the authorities. Our respondents are not social activists in the commonly circumscribed understanding of the term in scholarly literature on social movements. They do not actively coordinate mobilisation of activism in public arenas; neither are they directly confrontational with state authorities. In addition, they do not focus on a single issue, or adhere to a coherent plan of action. One way in which the Chinese Christians respond to the social injustices and suffering they witness around them is to voice them in social media. In doing this, they are building fellowship and solidarity by getting responses/agreements from other fellow Christians (and sometimes non-Christians as well). All our interviewees had no desire to translate such online critical voices into actual physical protests or demonstrations. In this sense, they did not wish to arouse the attention of the authorities. However, by not openly talking about "politics" and "sensitive issues" or mobilising activism on social media, this does not mean that our respondents are all non-political or frightened by state repressive measures such that they fall into a state of apathy and inaction. Many of them are very much socially engaged, in the workplace, community development work, and everyday life, without explicitly engaging in open social activism or large-scale social movements. Even so, their use of social media allows them to continue to spread Christian ideas and ideals, while hoping to change their acquaintances in various social contexts and, eventually, the wider society.

4 Tending the garden

Christianity in the workplace

Religion and the workplace

Like many young Christian professionals based in the cities, Wang, a doctor from Kunming, the capital of Yunnan province, did not come from a Christian family. Wang was introduced to Christianity while he was still a student in the university and got baptised after graduation. He strongly felt that his religious faith had been an important factor behind his career choices. After a stint as a junior doctor in the hospitals, Wang decided to work for a foreign NGO which partnered with the local government in providing medical care to the needy in Yunnan rural areas. When we asked him if one's religion and occupation should have a clear dividing line, Wang said, "I personally feel that religion and occupation do not have any clear division. I said that because my own religious belief has played a large role in my career choice".

In this chapter, we explore how Chinese Christian employees view work and the workplace through the lens of their religion, and how they seek to influence the broader society, in a highly restrictive religious domain in China. Our respondents wished to address the perceived moral problems which were prevalent in the society, through efforts to transform the workplace and their non-Christian colleagues. We argue that Christian employees did not see a clear boundary between the "religious" and the "secular" in the workplace. At the same time, they discursively constructed a distinction between their own Christian work ethos and that of their non-Christian colleagues. Most regarded the workplace to be an important arena for the concrete expressions of their Christian faith and values in everyday life. In doing so, they sought a moral transformation of the workplace as a way to transform the wider society with Christian values. In this regard, we argue that these Christians were engaging in a kind of religious social engagement. To recall, by "religious social engagement", we mean the efforts by religious individuals and groups to engage with social issues. They seek to readdress these issues, by engaging in activities that might or might not involve widespread and coordinated mobilisation efforts. We suggest looking beyond the common approaches of examining religious organisations' philanthropic and charitable activities, and their mobilisation in civil society. Some of these activities might be conducted in ways that are non-obtrusive and non-antagonistic in their interactions with controlling state institutions. We argue that, by examining this kind of activities as social engagement in everyday Christianity, in this case, in the workplace, we are able to better understand how Christianity can continue to experience a rapid growth in China. This rapid growth happens in the context of the deepening political authoritarianism, curtailment of an emerging civil society, and a tighter surveillance and control of Christianity by the Chinese authorities. By discursively construing work as service, Christian employees seek to change what they regard as unethical behaviour in the workplace, with the broader aim of addressing the perceived moral malaise inflicting the society at large.

"People Will See How You Walk Before They Believe What You Talk".

The above comment was made by Andy, an engineer working in a software company in the southern city of Shenzhen during the time of our interview. Andy's family had migrated to the United States when he was in high school. When he was growing up, some Christians had tried to introduce the Gospel to him and his family. At that time, he did not embrace the faith as he was an atheist. When Andy first started work in the Silicon Valley, some of his Christian colleagues and acquaintances began to introduce him to Christianity. He started to be open to the Christian faith only when he worked with some Christian businessmen whom he described as "Christians who lived out their faith". He was quite impressed when Christian colleagues confessed how God was a constant presence in their life, and he finally decided to become a Christian when he met a friend whom he felt lived an authentic and exemplary Christian lifestyle.

Andy's family's exposure to Christian faith influenced their lifestyle and resulted in them prioritising their Christian faith in their family, work, and other areas of life. This constant exposure to Christianity coincided with a period in his life when he was also "going through a lot of thinking". Eventually he came to realise that "there are something out there, that's beyond human power". The pivotal moment came when Andy's friend from mainland China invited him to a seminar given by a visiting Chinese Canadian scholar, whose talk touched him deeply. For him, Christianity was "for real":

> And also because of my friends with all their life examples, I knew the faith was for real, was something that was not just on paper, somehow that night I was so compelled, and I accepted the Lord that evening.

Soon, Andy started looking for a church, as this was to him the expected next step to take: "That's what I heard in America, if you believe this, you need to go to a church". Eventually, he found an Asian-American church in Berkeley where his parents whom he visited every weekend lived.

When Andy lost his job in the United States, he had the opportunity to relocate to China to work in a foreign software company. This also offered Andy a chance to evangelise in his country of origin. "And that's why I realised that the Lord has prepared me all these years, for me to go back to China". In his Shenzhen company, Andy started a Bible study group which met during the lunch hours. A few of the group members were already Christians when they joined the company, but some of them became Christians when they were influenced by their Christian colleagues. "It was over the years that I began to see how God had actually prepared me for Shenzhen, because it is right next to Hong Kong, so I would go to Hong Kong to do bible study". Andy's experience reveals how important the workplace is for evangelism among Chinese Christians. Many strive to be role models for the faith in their respective workplaces, as they interact with non-Christian colleagues and engage in workplace evangelism. At the same time, Chinese Christians, like Andy, are constantly negotiating the institutionally imposed boundaries that separate religion from other social domains, and face challenges in expressing their faith in the workplace. Over the past two decades, with the rapid rise of Christianity in China, it has prompted much research into various aspects of the phenomenon. Comparatively fewer studies have been conducted on how Chinese Christian employees view their work and workplace, the impact of religion on their relationship with non-Christian colleagues, and the challenges of integrating faith into the work domain.

Employees of a "different kind" *(linglei)*

It is important to recall that Christians—both Protestants and Catholics—comprise only a small percentage of China's population. Their numbers are also small compared to adherents of other religions such as Buddhism, Islam, and Daoism. With Christianity as a minority religion, this would mean that, except for those who work in Christian organisations, most other Chinese Christians work in an environment where most of their colleagues are non-Christians. This also means that the Christian employees' endeavour to integrate faith and work can potentially be fraught with tension and challenges. This is partly due to their small numbers, and partly because of a strong sense among Christian workers that their religious values distinguish them from the non-Christians. This is reflected in the experience of Linda from Wenzhou, who was enrolled in an independent seminary at the time of our interview:

> After graduation, I did an internship as a customer service officer at a hotel. My job was to serve patrons, and how I mix my faith with my job is that I make sure that at the very least, my service attitude on the surface must be thoughtful and attentive. Often, there are people who use underhand means behind customers' backs. For instance, if a customer was being rude, the waiter might be revengeful and add stuff into the customer's food before serving. When I witnessed all these, I really pitied the customer. The job was pressurising, because the customers are mostly rich people. However, if a Christian waiter is met with the same situation, he would not do the same, he would not do the same to you just because you have offended him.

Research from Australia has found that managers and professionals regard spiritual self-disclosure as a taboo and a stigma, and risk being perceived by their colleagues as "being on the outer edge", namely, marginalised from the social, cultural, and spiritual identity of the organisation (Crossman 2015). Such sentiments are shared by many respondents who regard themselves as qualitatively different from their non-Christian colleagues. For them, religious self-disclosure and expressions in the workplace can be simultaneously uplifting and challenging. For one of our interviewees, Andy, the IT specialist, his feeling of being different was supported by his Christian principles and what he termed "proper outlook". As he confessed,

> I feel that faith has allowed me to have a proper outlook of the world. I will have my principles and not drift about in the world. I know how to do the right things. For work, I feel the need to do things in a principled manner, and to put in my best effort.

Wang, the doctor based in Kunming, related how in his previous work in the hospital, he sometimes felt his colleagues regarded him as a "different kind" (*linglei*), a term which might carry a deviant undertone, because his behaviour and values often differed from theirs. Thus, the boundary between Christians and non-Christians seems to be drawn not just by the Christians, but also by the non-believers, in the workplace. As Wang noted, this supposed difference might have both positive and negative implications for workplace relations:

> In the hospital I was the only Christian. From my actions and the things that I say, they would have guessed that I am different from them. Some were accepting and found nothing wrong with that. But some would hang out less with you, thinking that you are different from them. However, there were still some who felt that I was nice to hang out with as an individual, and sometimes felt a little curious which prompted them to interact with me more, to learn more about my religion. So, there are differing attitudes from different groups of people.

When asked to elaborate on how being a Christian distinguished him from his colleagues, Wang emphasised that as much as possible he would make decisions "that are in accordance with Bible teachings". He was fortunate that his superior generally accepted his reasons for not doing things which contravened his religious principles. Wang gives an example whereby the hospital authorities directed the doctors to make fake diagnoses of patients and cases that did not exist, to improve the hospital's rankings by the health authorities. Wang explained to his supervisor that this contradicted his Christian values, but also indicated that he would contribute to the hospital in other ways. Fortunately, his superior saw that his attitude "was satisfactory" and "had trust in him", agreeing that he did not have to participate in the proposed scheme. This episode gave Wang the confidence "that there is power in religious belief". Similarly, another of our interviewee, Anne, who worked in the software industry in Shenzhen, partly attributed her positive work attitude when encountering difficulties to her faith:

> When I face difficulties at work, I often consult the Bible. Before, I might not know how to solve the problems. After I started believing in Jesus, I have become more demanding towards my work, because I feel that I cannot be the same as others.

According to Hui Wen, a sales executive, Christian workers tended to be more accommodating and understanding:

> Some non-Christians like to grumble and complain. For example, they might be dissatisfied when the boss gives the year-end bonus, saying that this year's bonus doesn't match last year's, or they will compare who gets more and less. But for us [Christians], we tend to be more understanding. I may feel that it's ok to have a bit less bonus, because business this year hasn't been good, and this is helpful for the boss's business. Or, when we encounter some minor problems, we will try to be more accommodating, and to touch others with our loving care. Some non-Christians have bad habits, after arriving they will first make coffee, surf the internet, and start their work in the afternoon. We will focus on doing our job well first thing in the morning.

Thus, Christian employees often construct boundary between themselves and non-Christian colleagues in their identity. They engage in a moralistic discourse that portrays themselves as embodying "correct" and more "positive" values. At the same time, these were also the values that were deemed lacking in the workplace and the wider society. They believed that it was the difference in their work attitude and their values that allowed them to showcase their faith to their non-Christian colleagues. They hoped that this would create a work culture that was imbued with Christian ethics. For Christian workers who find themselves in a workplace with a predominantly Christian workforce, the sharing of a common religion is the single most important element that contributes to these workers' sense of workplace well-being. Mary, one of our interviewees, was previously working as an accountant in a state-owned enterprise before her current job of teaching Chinese to foreigners in an international school. She worked in an environment where religion was taken seriously and expressed openly by colleagues. This presented a huge contrast to her previous work experience. It is not that the Christian workplace is devoid of problems. However, sharing a common religion contributes significantly to a strong sense of bonding between colleagues. It also provides moral resources for them to manage employees, and face difficulties together, in a more consensual and supportive way:

> When you encounter difficult problems, you will be able to share them with sisters-in-Christ, and they will even join you in prayers as well. One will always encounter difficulties in life. Regardless of work or daily life, there are bounds

> to be trials that one must go through. I have been in this sector for about 10 years, there are many problems which we face every day. It does not mean that we as a Christian school do not encounter any problem. We too have our own problems, and some of them are not small either. But the biggest difference is that we will be able to find someone to share and to pray for you. The difficult thing is life is not about the obstacles we face; it is more about the support and encouragement that the people by your side provide.

Sharing a common religion might contribute to the building of trust, and, hence, facilitate the cultivation of socially and commercially beneficial relationships with one's colleagues and business acquaintances. Hui Wen notes how her work performance has actually improved after she decided to focus more on her clients' needs instead of on her sales figures. For her, since becoming a Christian, this change in priority had unexpectedly improved her work performance. When her clients experienced her good and sincere service, many of them then introduced Hui Wen to their relatives and friends. For Simon, a Kunming-based teacher, Christians tend to be more trustworthy, compared to non-Christians. A Christian's ability to inspire trust (cf. Tong and Yang 2016) in others is good not only for sealing business deals but also motivating workers and establishing collegial atmosphere in the workplace. When asked how important religious faith is in the workplace, Simon opined:

> It's very important. First, it's trust. Because you will realise that in general among business people, many are not trustworthy. There are also many who want to get close to you through the faith. But to me, I might not interact with them often on a daily basis, but in times of real trouble, we are willing to help others, including in business. Workers may judge whether the company's boss, if he is profit-minded or really cares for the workers. While a company seeks profits, it should also look after the workers ... When one interacts with colleagues as a Christian, people will get along better, there is greater efficiency in discussing things.

In general, Christian employees believe that trust as social sacred leads to a transformation of work such that morality is reintroduced into work, and it carries the sacred value that work is designed to be in the bible. However, Christians can also experience a conflict between their Christian values and their work when certain aspects of their work are contrary to their Christian teachings, such as when the work becomes so demanding and pressurising that it competes against their time for their prayer, Bible study, with family, and other Christians, or when their bosses require them to do things which are contradictory to their Christian ethics. In such cases, work can be seen as a competitor of their Christian practices, rather than an alignment with their Christian worldview. In addition, Christians can also be vulnerable to exploitation as employers may think that they will accept any amount of work since they are expected to be kind and generous, and not complain.

A phrase that emerged constantly among Christian employees is "witnessing for the faith" (*wei xinyang zuo jianzheng*) at the workplace. It is through the expression of faith in their daily life and workplace that Christian employees often merge the "religious" and the "secular" (*shishu*). Commenting on how Christians should not be just "Sunday Christians" but should be religious exemplars in the normal workday, one of our interviewees, Kexin, a Kunming-based lawyer, believed that in this way Christians could evangelise to their colleagues:

> Your church life is different. But it doesn't mean we have to separate them, to the point that your Monday through Saturday is different from your Sunday. Why do you do that? Shouldn't your faith be a consistent route? But once more and more brothers and sisters realise that it is important to have faithful life even throughout the week, it would make such a difference in the sense that people began to look at our faith differently. They will not just think that you are the ones only do something special on Sundays, on all the other days you are the same as me. Maybe some of us are not as good as you. But now they see difference, they see these people they do live a different life. They don't try to please the boss, for example, they don't bribe others. And they come to work on time. They don't steal company's money, and they don't steal company's time. People normally may not steal money, but most people steal time. But these people [Christians] are solid. These people we need to respect. I think it would play a very significant role in evangelism, especially in Chinese culture.

Why do these Chinese professionals desire to integrate faith and work, or, more generally, seek to dissolve the distinction between the so-called "religious" (*zongjiao de*) and the "secular" (*shisu de*)? To answer this, we have to consider their view on the meaning of work.

Work as "service"

> I feel that, compared to when I just graduated, I understand more what I actually want in life, and how to do better in my job. The faith has really been a profound influence on me, and such deep influence also affects my subordinates. Yes ... just as how Jesus has influenced me, I influence my subordinates and those around me.
>
> (Yaqiong, Shenzhen)

Conversion to a new religion often brings about a sense of radical break with the past. One respondent said that her "thinking has changed" (*sixiang gaibian le*), while another mentioned that Christianity could "broaden one's horizon" (*shiye kaikuole*). Wenming, a marketing executive in Kunming, shared how becoming a Christian had motivated him to aspire towards a life of sanctity in accordance with biblical teachings, thus affecting a profound discontinuity with his past behaviour:

> After becoming a Christian, I felt that the Lord's intention was for us to be kind or perfect, to aspire toward sanctity. Because these are wonderful

> things, I aspire to achieve these. The Bible tells us, we must love one another. Maybe there is too much lacking and imperfection in my life, I have this wish to cultivate sanctity in my life according to what the Bible proclaims.

Zhiqing, our respondent who was a teacher, related that one big difference between being a Christian and her previous irreligious life was that "there is something in life to look forward to and that there is more hope in life". She further elaborated:

> We were always sad and dull previously. We brood about having lousy parents, lousy jobs, we felt that there was no meaning in life. However, after becoming a Christian, I feel that life is more fulfilling and become more hopeful (*shenghuo geng you yiyi, geng you xiwang*). I was able to gain different perspectives (*buyiyang de quandian*). I feel that your working attitude will change because of your own character, you will also become more proactive.

This sentiment of rupture and change featured prominently among the Chinese professionals in our interviews, when they related their views towards their work. First, the trope that was frequently mentioned by respondents in relation to work was "to serve" (*shifeng*). For them, work was not just a source of livelihood, but, more importantly, it provided an opportunity to serve God and the society at large. James, a software engineer in Shenzhen, described this transformation:

> Before, we thought that we only work for ourselves. However, two weeks ago, we went to a seminar, the teacher mentioned that actually we are working full-time. Because we are working, so we are employees. So if we work well, put in our best effort, to help others along as we work, we also serving the Lord ... I used to have the attitude of only doing the best for myself. When I was doing too many things and got irritated, my attitude would be quite negative. But if you believe in the Lord, even though this negativity could still be present to some degree, I feel I am uplifted. In the beginning you can't handle the pressure from work, but now, this limit of yours can increase a little, and you can endure.

Many respondents revealed how they, prior to embracing Christianity, usually viewed work as numbing. They often had to navigate poisonous workplace relations that sapped their morale and energy. Converting to Christianity had profoundly transformed their experience of work and the workplace. They shared about having acquired more positive attitude towards their work and their colleagues as they embraced a new outlook in life and made changes to their behaviour. As Mary, the respondent who was a teacher, said, "it is the same when it comes to work, when you become more proactive, you will engage yourself to do more things. I feel that the biggest change is the attitude to dare to challenge things". This transformation of work attitude does not mean that there are no longer problems in the workplace for the Christian workers. In fact, it could result in new social tension and ethical uncertainty. For example, Lee, McCann, and Yuen's (2012) survey of 119 Chinese business leaders found that when faced with challenging situations, the business leaders' responses inclined towards two types. The first type of response was a resolute rejection of morally questionable business practices from the perspective of Christian ethics. They did not try to change such business practices in the short term. The other main type of response was to compromise certain Christian values so that they might continue to do business in China. The tension between these two possible responses was also reflected in the case of Weixiong. Holding an executive position meant he was concerned about his company's profit levels, for the "main goal of a business is profit, to make money". After becoming a Christian, Weixiong increasingly found instances of conflict between his Christian values and business practices, and this conflict would not disappear. "Once you have this religious faith", he says, "you may encounter different tests and seductions, and you will use some Christian standards as basis of your judgement".

Another of our interviewees, Eleanor, came from a Christian family, and had worked in a Christian media company upon graduation from college. After a couple of years of film production and editing, she left the media company to work in a private education and training institution. For Eleanor, the workplace in her first job was comparatively less complicated compared to the second job, as "almost everyone was a Christian" and most shared the view that doing their respective jobs well was part of living out their Christian life. Eleanor's second job was a very different workplace environment. Her Christian faith often put her in situations where she had to constantly ponder the appropriate actions to take that would not compromise her Christian values, as she interacted with her superiors and colleagues. Below are excerpts from our interview with her:

US: Were there instances when what your boss told you to do went against your own belief, and you would say that because you were a Christian, and to do such things was inconsistent with your belief, so you were unwilling to do it?

ELEANOR: Yes, there were. I would say that the beginning is very important. In the first three months in my new job, I had left a very strong impression on my boss, that he knew what I would do and what I would not do; when I would say no to him. At first, I thought he didn't like me, because he had rarely encountered such kind of person. However, it turned out okay since he was quite satisfied with what I had done. So, there was a balance. Six months later, we had a chat. He asked me how it was going on. But at that time, he felt that how could my personality be like this, that I could be so straight-forward and dared to say no. However, it may be because I had done my work well, that was why he said he would give me another chance. Then I passed the trial period.

US: Can you give an example?

ELEANOR: In fact, there were many. For instance, it was a natural thing that to tell a white lie might resolve some embarrassment. But I would not do so. Instead, I would choose to tell the truth. Then of course he would not be very happy. However, you can only tell a person's true heart in the long run. Subsequently, he recognised the things I did. What is amazing is that he trusted me very much, he was very willing to listen to my proposals on many things. He thought that my ideas were always quite fair.

Eleanor's experience reveals the difficulties and dilemmas of working in an environment when one belongs to a minority faith. Indeed, being a Christian in a predominantly non-religious or even atheistic environment can result in ostracisation, marginalisation, and unwanted attention. As discussed before, Christian employees may feel that they are regarded by their non-Christian colleagues, sometimes negatively, as of a "different kind" (*linglei*). What most of our respondents emphasised was that, when faced with a negative or hostile work environment, they often had to rely on their religious faith to provide ethical guidelines and strength to meet the challenges. An example they related was alcohol consumption when socialising with one's superiors and colleagues. Susan was a manager's assistant who was a teetotaller for religious reasons. During company meals, she had to constantly make her colleagues accept her preference of not drinking alcohol with sensitivity:

> Whenever we have a gathering, together with my bosses, the whole division would hang out together for a meal and of course there would be alcohol involved. Because I work in the engineering section, there were only two girls to begin with, but I was the only one left as another went on maternity leave. As per social stereotype, with you being the girl, you would have to be the one to sit beside the manager and drink with him. That was when I told him that I am a Christian, and my religion forbids me to drink. They kept pressurising me to drink and so I had to stand my ground until they finally agree out of respect. Eventually they replaced alcohol with Sprite. And when you drink with them, you had to drink the whole cup in one gulp. While they drank white wine, I would have to down cups of Sprite one after another. Because of all these, *I felt reluctant to go to work as well. I feel that all these are not too good* and it might even be better if I work somewhere else.

Despite the challenges in working non-Christian workplace, Christian employees tend to interpret their desire to inspire a more positive mindset among colleagues as "providing witness" (*zuo jianzheng*) for their faith, and as "serving the Lord" (*shifeng zhu*). What does "service" and "to serve the Lord" entail? Concretely, they entail bringing the right (i.e. Christian) values to the workplace. In a society where the cultivation of good personal relationship (*gao guanxi*) with one's superiors and acquaintances is essential for one's career advancement,

Anne emphasised fairness, equality, and transparency in her work instead. In addition, she lamented that these values were not usually found in the workplace:

> Before, I had to conduct inspection, and felt that there should not be favouritism, and should treat everyone the same (*yishi tongren*)! It doesn't matter if you are a superior or a normal worker. This is a small matter, but I felt everyone should receive equal treatment. I strove for fairness, justice, and transparency.

For the Christian employees, who express and integrate faith and work couched in terms of "service", they hoped to transform people's values and the work culture. Ultimately, they aimed to embed Christian values in the wider society (cf. Wielander 2009). For these evangelical Protestants, the view of work as service dissolved the boundary between the secular work/workplace and religious life. Their desire to "provide witness for the faith" in the workplace was motivated by what they perceived as the main problem in the contemporary society, namely, the decline of morality. With the rapid social transformations which accompanied China's transition to a market-oriented society, personal and public morality has suffered. Many of our respondents worried that people are now overwhelmingly obsessed with the pursuit of personal gains and wealth. Simon, the Kunming teacher, opined:

> After the reforms, people come to have differing views on many issues. But in general, people acknowledge the economy as the main driving force, and early on, people were just focused on making money. But right now, even though people are generally more well-to-do and financially stable, their moral values have declined. From what I understand, young people nowadays also have some bad feelings about the society, and they do not have strong values to guide them. This has resulted in immoral acts happening within their circle, affecting themselves, their family, their career, which is definitely a negative impact on the society. And I am worried about that. Therefore, when people with Christian faith stand up in society, this will have positive impact, and I believe that society will then experience positive development.

Subsequently, for Christian employees, the everyday work environment is where China's moral crisis manifests in stark terms, and where they feel motivated to act in ways that might bring about a moral transformation, albeit little by little. They rely on religious values to guide their behaviour. As Weixiong, our respondent, noted, "Because we can provide witness for the faith during work, and even to spread the gospel, so I feel that it's very good, to be able to do one's work and the Lord's work". China is suffering from a moral crisis, and religion—Christianity in particular—is seen as a front of ethical principles to tackle widespread social ills. Adopting the view of religion as everyday practice, the Christian workers' discourse of work as "service" entails both being "servants" of God in the workplace and engaging in efforts to transform the society. Consequently, this dissolves the conceptual distinction between the "secular" and the "religious".

"Subtle infiltration": social media and workplace evangelism

We have discussed above about the Christian employees' desire to be a role model in the workplace, in order to influence their colleagues with Christian values, and shape workplace culture. The study's respondents stressed that they would refrain from open evangelism and prefer to influence their non-Christian colleagues in subtle ways. Apart from striving to be ethical employees, many respondents consider the social media as another important means for evangelism and spreading Christian values in the workplace. The use of social networking sites has become an integral part of our respondents' lives, including their religious pursuits. A typical example is Wen, our respondent, who is a woman in her early 20s. She shared her baptism experience in our interview with her:

> I posted my baptism pictures on QQ, and everyone was able to view them, as I did not set any restrictions. Many of my former classmates asked me, what are you doing, because there was a certificate. I told them that I was baptised. Then they asked me why I needed to be baptised? What is baptism? I told them that it's a procedure to becoming a Christian. They then asked me why I believe in Christianity, you are a Chinese and you still believe in it? Two days after I saw the comment, I told them that this is my choice and they have to respect that. After that one friend told me that she hoped that I could bring her to Christianity as well.

Anne, from Shenzhen, used the phrase "subtle infiltration" (*shentou*) to describe the preferred method:

> I will be subtle in Weixin [WeChat], not to proclaim that I am a Christian in an outright manner ... This kind of influence, it's a little by little, and slowly seeps into your consciousness. Then, you will ask me one day, you believe in this, right? And when you ask about the story of Jesus, I can then tell you loudly his story.

This method of subtle evangelism is possible on social media like WeChat because one's "friends" on the app include non-Christians. When someone posts some Christian content on WeChat, some non-Christians may become interested and respond to the post. Lily, our respondent who was a teacher in Kunming, described how this subtle evangelism works:

> There are also non-believers that are hidden somewhere in the group. One of them is actually a Buddhist. I feel that it is alright and it is actually very good. We can try to influence him with what we are doing. He might be thinking, 'let's see how long you all can last with this, it might just be a

> one-time thing for a short whole.' But in fact, we are going to do this for 10 over years. I do not know when he will convert and believe in God, but I will pray for him.

James, from Shenzhen, observed:

> When some people share some good things, I will share them in my other networks, or I will "like" and "support" on WeChat. I always do such things. Others may not know I am a Christian, but will ask, do you believe in this? I will then tell them indirectly.

Some respondents underscored the need to be subtle in their evangelism in social media, to avoid "scaring" others away. As one of them noted,

> Actually you want to share with them but you are worried that your evangelism will create negative feelings in them. If I am too keen, they will be frightened, and will be unwilling to come for activities. So don't be too straightforward, show concern for them bit by bit in their daily life, you can't rush things.

While many respondents view social media positively for its potential to facilitate evangelism in the workplace, some express a more cautious attitude and highlight its limitations. For Andy, social media like WeChat and QQ are regarded more as an effective tool for communicating with friends, colleagues, and family members in an environment where mobile phone usage is very widespread. He said, "To me, [these social media] are just a tool. I usually don't intentionally use QQ or WeChat to tell others about the gospel. Very little".

Partly due to their awareness of the political sensitivity of religion in China and partly due to their own personal preference for privacy, some respondents are more ambivalent about using social media as a means for evangelism among colleagues. There are also concerns that a more enthusiastic evangelism among one's circle of colleagues who are on one's social networking sites might put strain on friendship. Wang, when asked if he used social media to share religious material among friends and colleagues, expressed his concerns and how he was still trying to negotiate the travails of social media:

> If I do have some thoughts and feelings, I may put them in the private domain, and will not necessarily share them with others. I want to avoid putting pressure on my non-Christian friends, and not let them think that I am evangelising openly through social media. I don't quite like to do this, and in any case I want to maintain our friendship. They do know me and actually many friends know that I am a Christian, and I really treasure maintaining our relationship. But at the same time, I also hope that they will get to know about the faith. So, I am still exploring what's the appropriate way.

While Christian employees recognise social media as important tools for religious communication and practice in the workplace, they serve to complement, and would not replace, face-to-face interactions. Meanwhile, Christian employees assiduously avoid online discussion of "sensitive" and "political" issues, due to widespread perception of the ruling Communist Party's online surveillance and intolerance of dissent.

Conclusion

The Christian employees whom we interview tend to view the society as experiencing a moral decline. This view, in turn, reinforces their sense of being different and legitimises their effort in changing society, through influencing their colleagues and changing the workplace culture. At the individual level, Chinese Christians employees often strive towards the ideal of expressing their faith more holistically and, in turn, reinforce the religious values that form the basis of their ethical system (Giacolone and Jurkiewicz 2003). However, there are challenges. Chinese Christian employees' merging of religion, work, and other aspects of their daily life happens in a sociopolitical context, where Christians still constitute a small religious minority, and where Christianity can still be deemed a highly sensitive cultural and political issue, by many believers and non-believers alike.

Given the current focus on Chinese Christian entrepreneurs in the scholarly literature, one of the questions our study seek to answer is whether the experiences of the Christian employees are similar to, or different from, that of the entrepreneurs. Our findings suggest an important commonality: many, in both groups, strive to spread the gospel to non-Christians in the workplace and the wider society, and wish to express their religious faith more openly in their work life. This is not surprising, given that the two groups are broadly evangelical in their religious orientation and are embedded in similar political and societal context. There are, however, important differences. Compared to the Christian employees, the Chinese Christian bosses and entrepreneurs are much more capable of shaping the workplace culture to make it more aligned with Christian values. Many are also able to proselytise, to varying degree of success, among the employees who work for them. Additionally, some highly successful Christian entrepreneurs are able to rely on their wealth, influence, and high social status to work closely with government officials and agencies in their philanthropic, charitable, and "developmental" activities. However, this is not the case for Christian employees. Christian employees in China do not expect or demand their firms to create a conducive environment for them to practise faith–work integration. Neither are they relying on the government to sympathise with, or accept, their strongly held view that religion should not be confined to a narrowly demarcated "religious sphere" (*zongjiao jie*). These Christians are not engaging in "political merit-making" (Weller et al. 2017), meaning they are not cultivating favourable ties with party-state officials, for their social engagement. Rather, they are both aware and wary of the wider sociopolitical context, as they seek to practise religion in their everyday life in a more encompassing manner, including in the workplace.

At the individual level, our respondents often discursively construct a boundary between themselves and the non-Christians in the workplace, where they regard themselves as more motivated and understanding, having a more positive attitude towards work, and less corruptible. This discursive, self-othering is double-edged. On the one hand, it enables the Christians to construct a distinctive workplace and social identity, one that is framed in religious terms. On the other hand, this risks their being negatively seen by non-Christian colleagues as belonging to a "different kind" (*linglei*). Thus, this may accentuate the social gulf and tension that might have already existed between the Christian and the non-Christian employees. While Christian employees might wish to be role models in the workplace, many are also aware of the need to remain "subtle" in expressing and propagating their faith. One "subtle" way of doing so is through the use of social media. In other words, in a broader restrictive political and cultural environment, they constantly experience a tension between their strong desire to express their faith more openly and the need to sometimes avoid explicit religious expressions in the workplace.

Social change, as expressed by the respondents, entails the moral transformation of the society. In other words, they consider the transformation of the workplace to be a part of their effort to transform the society, in accordance with Christian values. From their evangelical standpoint, their ultimate aim is the Christianisation of China. Some might question whether the lack of a more direct effort to change social structures, or of a more explicitly expressed political vision on the part of the Christian employees, could be regarded as seeking social change. We argue that we need to broaden our conception of social change and social engagement, particularly, to pay attention to unobtrusive social engagement. The Christian employees' attempt to change the moral climate of the workplace and the society represents an effort, in a relatively unobtrusive manner (especially in the political climate of China), to change society in the long run. This attempt is based on a religious vision, often without explicitly referencing the "political", as it is commonly understood. One reason is that, for these Christians, the "political" is already subsumed under, or encompassed by, their religious vision.

Unlike the intellectuals in the literature on "culture Christians" who engage in theological and theoretical debates over Christianity's role in China's social and moral transformation, Christian employees may be engaging in unobtrusive social engagement. How do they do so? Our respondents avoid the overt Christian mobilisation and activism in civil society, as documented in some existing studies on religion and social change in China. Their perception and experience of moral decline in society motivate them to seek moral and social transformation, not by open advocacy through civil society activism, but through influencing their colleagues and workplace culture. Many respondents consider their work to be a means for social transformation, as viewed in moral terms. For them, the workplace is an arena where Christian evangelism, the perceived moral decline of contemporary society, and supposed solution to the crisis are entangled, allowing for a distinct narrative and practice of Christian social engagement to emerge in China. Chinese evangelical Protestant employees rationalise this effort in terms of work, as a form of "service", to God, colleagues, and society.

Unlike the Christian entrepreneurs or Wenzhou "Boss Christians" described in the literature, Christian employees in our study do not enjoy the relative freedom and authority to openly express their faith in the workplace. Neither are they able to demand their secular firms, or appeal to the country's laws, to support their faith–work integration. In an authoritarian political context where civil society activism is curtailed, the workplace provides a relatively "safe" domain for Christian employees to engage in religious transformation of society, in less obtrusive and more subtle ways, outside the direct monitoring of the authorities. For these Christian employees, the cultivation of personal piety and engagement in subtle proselytisation in the workplace are not solely a matter of saving souls, but also transformation of the moral fabric of society.

5 Harvest of righteousness

Holistic development

The GMV in China

When the deadly earthquake struck the remote mountain regions of Sichuan on 12 May 2008, the foreign Christian NGO GMV (pseudonym) had already been involved in various community development projects in the province for 14 years. In the immediate aftermath of the disaster, the GMV was able to respond quickly to assist in the rescue, restoration, and reconstruction effort, in collaboration with local governments and civic organisations. An advanced GMV team arrived on 15 May in the city of Mianyang to set up the organisation's command posts in order to prepare for the arrival of medical relief and rescue workers sent by the organisation's Chengdu office. For the next two months, GMV workers toiled alongside local health, medical, and rescue personnel, as well as provided counselling to survivors and displaced people. For the subsequent restoration phase, the GMV set up the Mianyang regional office and signed a three-year memorandum of understanding with Beichuan County Health Bureau for medical and health development. During this phase, the GMV provided expert help with the rehabilitation treatment for victims of the earthquake, conducted rehabilitation training for local medical workers, and began to station a long-term teacher in Beichuan Middle School. In the following reconstruction phase, which started in 2009 (and is continuing at the time of writing), the GMV signed MOUs with several schools and educational institutions to provide teacher training. In addition, the organisation continued to partner with county governments, hospitals, healthcare centres and bureaus in poverty alleviation projects. As one GMV worker reflected, Beichuan was the city where "the Lord opened the door" for the group to reach new areas and peoples in the region.

This chapter presents a case study of the GMV to address the following questions: Given the Chinese government's increasingly strict regulations on the activities of civic and religious groups, especially foreign ones, how can foreign Christian groups, such as the GMV, continue to pursue their aims of transforming Chinese society, spreading Christian ideals, and seeking new converts? What kinds of discursive practices are Christian NGOs adopting to legitimise their development activities in the eyes of their own members, the broader Chinese public as well as an officially atheistic Chinese Communist Party? Conversely, in what ways is the authoritarian party-state mobilising and collaborating with these foreign Christian NGOs, while continuing to publicly adhere to its atheistic ideology? As we answer these questions, we do not presume at the outset that foreign religious NGOs, generally, and Christian ones, in particular, are either seeking to undermine or circumvent the authority of the party-state, or collaborate with it unwillingly or under duress. Neither do we assume that the expansion of space for civic groups in China and, in this case, for religious NGOs would necessarily pose a challenge to the party-state's legitimacy and its hold on power. Relatedly, we do not postulate an all-powerful government which has its tentacles grasping and manipulating all domains of Chinese society, such that the last resort of most civic groups is to constantly respond to its agenda and actions.

In the following sections, as a point of departure from the resistance and the accommodation approaches, we shall be using the global field framework, as elaborated in Chapter 2, to discuss the community development work of the GMV. We believe that the global field framework can offer fresh insights for a more comprehensive analysis of religious agents' activities in the charitable and development sector in China. Specifically, the global field framework allows us to examine how the religious beliefs, values, and motivations of the workers in a Christian NGO like the GMV have been able to contribute its resources in the pursuit of holistic development as a social sacred.

The GMV was headquartered in Hong Kong at the time of our research, with branches in 13 regional centres around the world, and ran projects in 13 sites in Sichuan, Yunnan, and Chongqing. For example, in Yunnan province, the GMV had a long-term team comprising speech therapists, dentists, nurses, and special education teacher who was based in the city of Liuku and who worked with children with disabilities. The medical doctors conducted surgeries and provided community-based rehabilitation. In 1996, the GMV worked with the Sichuan provincial government to conduct medical education, nursing training, and medical services in some counties. Since then, the organisation had sent teachers to various communities to teach English in hospitals and schools. In 1999, Zhaojue county, which was part of the Liangshan Yi Autonomous Prefecture, invited the GMV to establish a youth centre for vocational training and youth development. The vocational training included basic skills training such as carpentry, plumbing and electricity, agriculture, livestock, auto repair, sewing, embroidery, and weaving. The centre also conducted recreational activities such as sports, singing, and other cultural activities to help the youth to develop "holistically". The GMV, local government, and local community regarded these programmes as vital in addressing problems related to alcoholism, smoking, drug abuse, and poor hygiene.

Why did the local government and the local community choose the GMV, a foreign Christian NGO, to be involved in the post-earthquake relief work? One reason was historical. As mentioned, the organisation was affiliated to the British evangelical mission which had provided social services in Zhaojue and the surrounding regions in the 1940s. In the 1950s, following the establishment of the

Communist government in China, the foreign missionaries sent by the GMV were expelled from the country but left behind their legacy in the schools, hospitals, and pockets of Yi Christian communities they had established. It was due to these legacies and history that the GMV founder was able to re-establish connections with the local Yi people and local government in the early 1990s. The forefathers of the founder of GMV were well-known figures in the region. The GMV founder was able to enquire about possible collaboration in the proposed youth project and other poverty alleviation programmes. One veteran GMV volunteer recalled the founder's insistence on the need of Christian professionals to engage in development work, especially among the impoverished communities in remote parts of China:

> The founder of GMV had always challenged Christian professionals to engage in this humanitarian effort by reminding them about their stewardship. He taught them that as much as God has given them gifts, training and education, God's purpose for them is to share these gifts with the needy communities. The skills and education of Christians, like material wealth, are not for the sole possession of those who have them, but to share with the community. In the process of working among the impoverished communities, Christians then share their Christian values with the people through life examples of their actions, and attitudes of love and hospitality. In the founder's words, these values will then infiltrate the community, like a tea bag that is dipped into hot water, cumulating into a general embrace of the Christian values by the community.

According to Edwin, one of the earliest GMV volunteers who had visited Zhaojue seven times, the high unemployment rates among the local youths prompted the local government to invite the GMV to start a wide-ranging youth engagement programme. In the 1990s, while Edwin attended the Methodist Church in Singapore, he heard that the GMV was seeking volunteers to start the youth project among the Yi minority in Zhaojue. As the church at the time was considering sending missionaries to the so-called "unreached people", Edwin responded to the GMV's call to help start the youth programme in Zhaojue. He described the GMV's work as "sowing the seeds". Edwin emphasised that it was due to the convergence of interests of local community, the government, and GMV, in the broader pursuit of "poverty alleviation", that created favourable conditions for GMV to work in Zhaojue:

> In China, you really need government support, and if you're going to be in the public ministries, so at that point in time, China was *seeking outside help*, to overcome poverty, among the minorities in these remote places, under the title of Poverty Alleviation... The youth centre in Zhaojue was set up to provide training to misplaced youth ... the youths just went into a black hole, aimlessness, leading to a lot of vice, sex, drugs, etc. So that was one area which the government said "please help us" ... So [the GMV] sent multidisciplinary

> teams and they saw this was a sheep farming area, so they were able to mobilise sheep farmers from New Zealand to participate. The approach was to help communities and address their needs, to use *global expertise* to kick start their own economy, for education and training. [italics added]

As previously defined, the social sacred refers to an agglomeration of ideals which are widely shared among different social groups which are striving for attainment of common good of society. In this chapter we discuss how holistic community development has become a social sacred in China and how this has enabled the GMV, a foreign Christian international development NGO, to work together with the local governments. Historically, in China, religious organisations have been involved in areas such as elderly care, public health (e.g. AIDS and leprosy care), disaster relief and humanitarian work, poverty alleviation, literacy and education projects, and agricultural improvements. Particularly, some Christian groups and churches have stepped up their social engagement efforts over the past two decades. This was possible partly because of China's wish to create a so-called "harmonious society": a number of Protestant groups responded by spreading the Christian notions of love through charitable and philanthropic activities, participating in community development work, and publishing Christianity-related journals and books (Wielander 2011). An important Christian theological foundation of the social gospel is the Hebrew concept of *tsedekah* (charity) with its notion of social justice (Morris 1986; Poe 2012). Numerous passages in the Old Testament narrate how God shows consideration and provision for the poor by commanding the Israelites to show justice towards the poor and not be prejudiced towards the wealthy. For example, in Leviticus 19:15, "Do not pervert justice; do not show partiality to the poor or favouritism to the great, but judge your neighbour fairly". In another reference, in the Jewish festivals of the Jubilee Year and Year of the Sabbath, the Israelites were commanded by God to ensure a more equitable distribution of resources and provide for the poor,

> If one of your countrymen becomes poor and sells some of his property, his nearest relative is to come and redeem what his countryman has sold … If one of your countrymen becomes poor and is unable to support himself among you, help him as you would an alien or a temporary resident, so he can continue to live among you … If one of your countrymen becomes poor among you and sells himself to you, do not make him work as a slave.
>
> (Leviticus 25:25, 35, 39)

The Israelites were also to care for the orphans, widows, and the poor:

> At the end of every three years, bring all the tithes of that year's produce and store it in your towns, so that the Levites (who have no allotment or inheritance of their own) and the aliens, the fatherless and the widows who live in your towns may come and eat and be satisfied.
>
> (Deuteronomy 14:28–29)

Such biblical injunctions to help the disadvantaged is an expression of Christian charity (*caritas*). This is the very impetus for a group of medical professionals to establish the GMV in 1994. Its initial aim was to offer medical aid to the poor in southwestern China. Outsiders may not be aware that the GMV is affiliated with a well-known transnational Christian evangelical organisation that was first established around the mid-19th century in Britain with the goal of bringing the Gospel to China. Indeed, the GMV's founder is the direct descendant of the founder of this evangelical mission and had become its Director General in 1980. Currently, with the support of over 70 long-term workers and their families in China, the GMV has expanded its scope of work from medical aid to include youth work, livestock projects, English education, business training, and community development. Since the late 1990s right up till 2010, one of us had been a volunteer at the GMV and had been actively involved in English teaching, youth projects, and humanitarian relief work in Sichuan. Thus, we had been able to gain an insider's perspective of the GMV on community development. We had conducted semi-structured, formal, and informal interviews with the GMV leaders and workers. The interview data was checked and corroborated through our own knowledge and experience with the organisation. In addition, the organisation's website was an important source of useful information for our research. We had consulted the GMV's quarterly bulletins which were freely and publicly available online. Due to the politically sensitive nature of religious issues in mainland China, especially pertaining to the activities of foreign religious agents such as Christian NGOs, we had been careful in ensuring anonymity of our respondents by using pseudonyms and disguising certain identifiable background information.

In her study of Amity Foundation, a large government-affiliated Christian organisation in China, Carino (2016) examines how the party-state often "harnessed" religious organisations like Amity Foundation to address development challenges, such as rising wealth gap in society. The party-state's mobilisation has empowered FBOs and helped legitimise their social roles. At the same time, FBOs need to offer "visible, viable and replicable alternatives in their social practices that are firmly rooted in their faith, if they are to make any sustainable impact on the development debate". For the workers and volunteers in FBOs to pursue sustained social engagements, their activities need to be framed in religious terms. Christian development workers say their participation in humanitarian and development work, and acts of charity, ultimately flow from God's love and goodness, which motivate them to extend the goodness to the needy. Hirono (2008) describes how members of three international Christian NGOs working in ethnic minority communities are firm believers of the universality and superiority of their own values. By engaging the charitable and humanitarian work among the economically poor and materially deprived ethnic minority communities, they hoped to improve the lives in these communities. As for the GMV, it refers to ethos as the "Kingdom values", and its workers are asked to see the world and the people they work with through "Kingdom lenses". As one Sichuan site manager reflected:

> Can we see beyond the ragged clothes, gnarled hands and dirty faces into eyes of brothers and sisters created in the image of God? Can we look beyond

> the lack of formal education and Chinese language ability to understand the heritage of people into whose hearts the Lord has planted eternity? Can we gaze beyond the dirt floors, make-shift cupboards and fire pits to value the richness of a culture being redeemed by the Father?

For many GMV leaders and workers, their participation in helping the disadvantaged and marginalised populations in the ethnic minority areas of Southwest China is seen as practising "incarnational ministry". The term "incarnational ministry" means to immerse oneself in another culture and become like Jesus in that culture. The following section will elaborate on the incarnational ministry as an essential expression of the "Kingdom values" of the GMV.

Incarnational ministry: being Jesus to the needy

When GMV workers and leaders discuss incarnational ministry, they draw from the model of Jesus's ministry in the Bible. Their aspiration to live "incarnational lives"—to be Jesus to those among whom they live and work—is motivated by the biblical examples of Jesus demonstrating his love for people by walking amongst them, healing their diseases, chasing out demons from the demon-possessed, and comforting the afflicted. Wells (2017) describes eight characteristics of incarnational ministry: presence, attention, mystery, delight, participation, partnership, enjoyment, and glory. "Presence" alludes to physical presence with the people in the community (particularly those who are suffering). It involves being empathetic with their situation and conveying the presence of God to the people who otherwise do not know about God. The emotional attributes of "attention", "enjoyment", and "delight" demonstrate identification with the conditions and emotional experiences of the people. Lastly, "mystery" and "glory" are the characteristics of God which people can witness through the incarnational service of Christians. Thus, as Christians, many GMV workers identify Jesus as a model, and often emphasise that his ministry was to provide for the needy and marginalised to ameliorate their suffering. Jennifer, one of our respondents who was an English teacher from Singapore, quoted Luke 4:18 to describe what motivated her:

> The Spirit of the Lord is on me, because He has anointed me to preach good news to the poor. He has sent me to proclaim freedom for the prisoners and recovery of sight for the blind, to release the oppressed.

In her reflection via email exchanges with one of us, Jennifer emphasised that Jesus's incarnation and embodiment in the human form was for her one of the key theological foundations of incarnational ministry:

> From the scripture, we learn that Jesus is the embodiment in human form of God's nature, compassion and sacrificial love for the world. His disciples in the bible as well as Christians, are called to follow Jesus' model of ministry, a model which is characterised by the attributes of identity with the suffering of the

people and care and concern for the marginalised in society, such as the poor; widows; orphans and prostitutes. The implicit assumption of this form of ministry is that *by watching the actions and selfless love of Christians in their service to society, other people who are not believers will be able to witness the love of God and be moved by it*. This is shown in the bible verse John 1:14 which states "the Word became flesh, and dwelt among us" and in Jesus' proclamation of his identity in the bible, John 14:7, "If you really know me, you will know my Father as well. From now on, you do know him and have seen him."

At a deep and personal level, many GMV workers we interviewed mentioned the notion of "calling" in their explanation of their motivation to engage in community development work. For one of our respondents, Meihui, a full-time administrator of GMV, her intense dissatisfaction with her job prompted her to ask deeper questions about life's meaning and God's plan for her:

> My current role, I guess, started out about 9 years ago when I was working as a lawyer in a bank. And I had an early mid-life crisis, is the best way to describe it. When I just felt I was pretty much done with banking, which I never was very interested in any way. It was just a job. I just felt a certain panic that if I kept going, I would end up having a life which I was not fully satisfied with. So, I thought about leaving my job, knowing that if I really did something I did believe in, it wouldn't be in the field of finance. I would have to start from scratch. And when I came to a point, when I was willing, basically to throw away my career, I prayed and asked God to send me where He could use me. I was actually interested in things like humanitarian work and charity work, but I'm married, I'm stuck in Singapore, I can't just bunk off to Uganda or something. So, options were somewhat limited, and I heard about opportunities to serve in a Christian non-profit organisation. So, I made that switch 9 years ago.

For the Kunming-based Dr Wang, his "calling" is interpreted in terms of Christianity's distinction from other religions: Christianity is God's "calling" to mankind which Christians understand through His revelation ("基督教是一个天启的宗教"), whereas the origins of other religions stem from man's "calling" or "searching" for God. In this sense, Christian ethics acts as both moral constraints and the key moral force that motivates believers to live out a full Christian life. This is because they are called to embody God's love for all humankind. The understanding of one's calling to live a full Christian life underpins many of our interviewers' belief—including Dr Wang's—that Christianity, as a religion, is not only "personal faith"; it is inseparable from other domains of social, economic, and political life. As Dr Wang reflected:

> From the perspective of one's own cultural customs, I feel that religion in a personal matter, a personal faith. But ultimately one's life is inseparable from one's social groups, hence I feel that religion and society are intertwined in myriad ways.

Our GMV informants highlighted that when they gave to the needy, they were at the same time giving to Jesus and serving him. Many referred to Matthew 25:35: "For I was hungry, and you gave me something to eat, I was thirsty and you gave me something to drink, I was a stranger and you invited me in". The GMV workers considered engaging in charitable acts as an extension of their close relationship with Jesus and an imitation of Jesus's work among the marginalised and needy. While they generally took care not to engage in open evangelism, they hoped that due to the emphasis on holistic or "balanced" (*pingheng*) approach to health and well-being, recipients of their services would come to realise the importance of spirituality and eventually embrace Christianity. Grace, a doctor specialising in infectious diseases, characterises her community work in Sichuan as "pre-evangelism":

> There is religion involved, but there is no preaching involved. So, it is more like we want them to discover, and then they identify, and then they come back with questions. Or if we see there's an openness and interest, then you can do Bible studies or some Bible examples that are also helpful for development. My end result is not that they are evangelised, but it's like pre-evangelism. You must change the worldview and values first. Only if you have a changed worldview that you can accept the biblical truth... It's a very slow process, very long-term effects. So, to me I am doing pre-evangelism and just trying to change world views, so it's a transforming process.

As Tom, an architect in his 50s who had also lived in Zhaojue with his wife and two young children, said,

> We are not there to preach the gospel. We tell them upfront we will not preach the gospel openly... But if people asked us who we are, we are more than happy to tell them who we are, how we became Christians, how Christianity has changed our perspectives on life.

As an architect, Tom oversaw the construction of the youth centre in Zhaojue and helped to establish its programmes. He saw his presence in the community as serving two purposes: drawing upon Christian values to be a model for a new way of life, and build relationships and community. Tom hoped to demonstrate that how he and his family lived and treated one another was different from that of the locals. In this way, he hoped to encourage the latter to embrace new values, outlook, and behaviour with the goal of achieving a better life. All this should be done without open evangelism, and framed in terms of "change", "improvement", "hygiene", and "mindset":

> So, when they looked at us, they immediately can identify the difference. The way we live, the way we treat our children. When they come to our house, they look at the house, the way we keep our house. One simple

> example was this. In the Yi house, the toilet is detached from the main house. But when they came to my house and saw the toilet in the house, they were amazed. "How did you keep the smell away? How can you keep your house so clean? You guys don't seem to fall sick as easily, right? The way you communicate with each other shows a lot of respect, a lot of love for each other." Daily things like that, they can see the contrast. The way we carry ourselves with confidence, the way we talk.

Given a chance, Tom and the other GMV workers would explain with the local people the religious reasons behind their seemingly contrasting mindset and ways of living. They actively presented themselves as embodiments of the new way of life that the government and many local people sought to achieve through community development. As Tom insisted, the physical and aesthetics aspects of the youth centre building paled in significance to the new mindset, skills, and life skills that could be cultivated through the centre's programmes:

> The building will one day be torn down. I don't even care about building because it is just a place for us to do things. I speak from the perspective of the youth centre *as a model*. I will make this place so special that it will become the standard for everybody else. When you walk into the youth centre, immediately you can tell the difference. We have rules like you cannot spit, you cannot litter, you cannot bring your cows in, you cannot bring your horses in. They come to our offices, and they say, "Wow your office is different." So, these are some of the things that we do. Like I said, we are displaying what this community *can be*. And we're trying to *change their perspective*. That was my primary aim.

In summary, the incarnational ministry practised by GMV workers incorporates a holistic view of a person: physical, emotional, professional, and spiritual. The GMV advocates the idea that a Christian's profession is a calling from and service to God. A Christian life, including the professional life, should demonstrate the attributes of the nature of God. Furthermore, healing for the community does not just lie in physical, emotional, and psychological recovery. It is also spiritual healing, which is possible only when people are restored in their relationship and union with God. Therefore, the incarnational ministry merges the "sacred" and "secular", the mundane and spiritual. It advocates that the service and actions of the Christian should be consistent with the Christian belief and values.

Holistic development: global field perspective

At the time of this research, the GMV's widened scope of work includes community development, education, business training, youth work, and livestock projects. In recognition of the GMV's effort in improving the lives of the poor, one county in Sichuan conferred honorary citizenship on the organisation's founding president. In recent decades, both Catholic and Protestant Christian social teachings have placed greater emphasis on integrating gospel messages with social, political, and environmental issues. Modern Christian mission "has continued across an expanding range of modalities, from familiar agendas of proselytisation to diverse projects of development pursued through the institutional apparatus of NGOs" (Feener and Scheer 2018: 3). This means that, at least for some denominations such as the Evangelicals and the Catholics, their believers are often involved in projects for social transformation. For example, as part of global civil society, it is important for churches in Asia "to move in the direction of advocacy for social and environmental causes, and empower the communities at the grass-roots level for social transformation" (Wilfred 2014: 337–338).

This recent emphasis on holism in evangelisation can be traced at least to the Lausanne Convention promulgated at the International Congress on World Evangelisation in 1974 (Lim 2013). In an article published in the summer 2017 issue of the GMV's quarterly bulletin, the writer shares her thoughts on what she calls "holistic gospel". For her, the term has a biblical basis, particularly the passage in John 3:16: where the word "world" is translated from the original Greek word, ***kosmos***, which means the entire cosmos or whole of creation. According to the author, to be "reconciled" with God from a redemptive perspective entails all of God's creation. All Christians are responsible for the care of this creation. This interpretation of the holistic gospel demands that a Christian response to environmental crisis include attention to people, practise of charity, ecology, conservation, and the environment.

In relation to our global field model, another aspect of the broader context is the role of the national society in regulating religious activities in China. For example, in 2012 the State Administration for Religious Affairs issued "Advice on Encouraging and Regulating Religious Sector's Participation in Philanthropic and Charitable Activities". This was followed by the nationwide "Religious Charity Week". Many religious groups, under the exhortation of the party-state, organised public fundraising activities and publicised their commitment to provide social services. Meanwhile, international aid organisations and NGOs, which are integral constituents of the global civil society, arrived in China. This international aid is a result of the partnership between local governments and civic organisations. Despite this, both local and foreign faith-based charitable and humanitarian organisations often engage in uneasy negotiations with the state in a fledgling national civil society.

On 1 January 2017, a new law enhancing the authorities' power to manage the operations of foreign non-governmental organisations came into effect. Under this piece of legislation, all foreign NGOs are required to register with the State Council Public Security and Provincial Public Security bureau. Along these lines, the GMV website carried reports of the organisation's successful registration with the relevant provincial authorities in Sichuan and Yunnan, including a meeting held in June 2017 between the current director of the GMV and the head of the Yunnan Public Security Bureau's Foreign NGOs Regulation Office.

The Yunnan provincial government's report noted that the GMV director had expressed gratitude for the government's "timely assistance, effective legal guidance and warm services", promising that the GMV would continue to be "law abiding". Due to the slew of new measures and regulations implemented in recent years by the Chinese government, a GMV leader noted:

> We want to continue working with the Chinese government, but we recognize that official agreements with the government entities are increasingly difficult to obtain. New and creative services and partnerships are being explored. We continue in our commitment to work within China's legal framework.

Currently, many FBOs working with local governments on community development projects in China publicly downplay the "religious" aspects of their work. In our global field framework, this entails the need for religious agents or organisations to interact with the prevailing discursive and political environment of the national society and operations of other national civic groups. For example, Master Xing Yun, the founder of Foguang Shan, a prominent Buddhist group from Taiwan, mentions in an interview with the *New York Times* that the group's activities in China is not to spread Buddhism, but "only to promote Chinese culture to cleanse humanity" (Johnson 2017). For some Buddhists in China, the endemic social sufferings they witness in society motivate them to actively practise compassion in their daily life and engage in volunteerism as a form of this-worldly spiritualism. The Buddhists consider this kind of social engagement as part of humanistic Buddhism (*renjian fojiao*). Doing good works in society is understood by the Buddhists as part of practising gratitude and accumulating good karma that are necessary for one's spiritual cultivation (Kuah-Pearce 2014). The stated aim of Jinde Gongyi, a social services provider under the Chinese Catholic Patriotic Church, was "to promulgate the Church's excellent tradition for social services, strengthen the collaboration between the local church, various social groups and foreign grassroots organisations, to share resources, to benefit the people, and to facilitate society's *balanced development*" (italics added; see also Zhang 2008; McCarthy 2013). Note how this kind of discourse, which is present in different religious traditions, is very much in line with the current prevailing global development discourse that emphasises the ideal of "balanced" or "holistic" development. This ideal has been institutionalised through the practices of powerful international development agencies and NGOs which are participating in global civil society. Increasing numbers of religious groups are using the discourse of development in their approaches to tackle social and environmental problems. This is an important means for them to demonstrate their social relevance to governments and communities. In relation to sustainable development, for example, the United Church, Synod of Western Australia, proclaimed that nature is God's creation, hence, there is a need "to promote the responsible management, use and occupation of the earth by human societies" (Narayanan 2013: 133).

International development organisations may use the word "holistic" in their work, but they may hold different interpretations of the word. Writing for the GMV's bulletin, Linda, a former GMV's director of personnel, interpreted the word from "a scriptural view of man", man as a multifaceted being:

> Man was created in the image of God. Our first ancestor was made a "holistic" being, formed from the dust of the ground and God's breath of life; that reflects the nature of the Triune God. Ever since the day of creation, man has been a physical being, a mental being, an emotional being, a psychosocial being and a spiritual being. All these facets of humanity are interwoven and interrelated in such a way that each cannot be separated from the other. *In serving the holistic needs of the Chinese people, [the GMV] honours the lordship of Christ in all things.* In a world that is exceedingly individualised, compartmentalised and specialised, we seek to serve in *interdisciplinary* teams to achieve our goals of holistic care.

The emphasis on holistic development by religious agents, such as the GMV, partly draws on the recent trends on global civil society and the global discursive practice of development. Since the late 1980s, a new development paradigm on the global development front has started to focus on ethics and values. This new paradigm stipulates that the pursuit of economic wealth need not and should not be done at the expense of important aspects of human development (e.g. 1994 UNDP Human Development Report). This perspective broadens the scope of development beyond economic development to include social well-being, political and human rights, cultural identity and values, and environmental sustainability (Goulet 1988).

An illustration of how this new development paradigm has influenced the work of religious agents, such as the GMV, can been seen in a 2017 issue of its quarterly bulletin. The lead article in this issue highlights how the organisation's general programmes are broadly in line with UN goals, and discusses these programmes in relation to the United Nations Development Program (UNDP) Millennium Development Goals and the 2016 Sustainable Development Goals (SDGs). The article highlights that five of its major programmes in China mirrors 14 of the 17 SDGs, and reiterates GMV's commitment to sustainable development, poverty eradication, and provision of more opportunities to the underprivileged. The GMV's approach to holistic development is encapsulated in Figure 5.1.

Meanwhile, religious groups have increasingly been shaping the global development agenda. As Tomalin (2012: 699) notes:

> Much literature, therefore, reflects the global trend towards favouring faith-based contributions to development and the desire to bring faith to the fore following its earlier marginalisation in mainstream development discourse and policy.

Figure 5.1 The GMV's "holistic services".
Source: The GMV Bulletin online.

On the influence of religious discourse behind this shift, Thomas (2004) describes how the World Health Organization has re-defined health, well-being, and quality of life to include spiritual health. Rees has highlighted the "secular" and "sacral" as two main understandings of development. The secular perspective acknowledges religion's continuing relevance for all aspects of people's life in the contemporary world. This is also an important source of moral standards. In this view, religious traditions are important to development insofar as they may provide ethical frameworks for global capitalism. In short, religion can make global capitalism more "humane". This is a secular perspective "because even though religious traditions are active (and indeed important) in this development discourse, they are also subordinate to a larger more primary economic agenda" (Rees 2013: 271). This is arguably the approach that the Communist Party in China takes in the mobilisation of religious resources for development. On the other hand, the sacral perspective recognises how religious values, as a source of moral values, shape the very identification of the ends of development. The gradual shift in the global development paradigm, together with the actions of civil society groups in advocating for changes in the practices of international development agencies, has opened up a space for religious groups to play a more important role in framing the development agenda and make their presence felt in different communities engaging in the practical pursuit of development (Clarke 2008).

In tandem with the shifting global development paradigm, the so-called "Community Health Evangelism" (CHE) has been profoundly influential among some religious agents, such as evangelical Christian groups engaging in health and medical aspects of community development. Abbreviated as the CHE, the approach emphasises "empowerment", "holistic" development, and leadership training, as described in the website of Medical Ambassadors:

CHE equips individuals to be independent workers and evangelists in their communities. CHE's training strategies that create this dynamic include:

- Empowering people to do things for themselves. This liberates locals from the bondage of the welfare mentality.

- Reaching the whole person. Some mission programmes deal solely with the spiritual dimensions and ignore physical needs; others address only the physical. CHE addresses both.
- Equipping leaders with skills to see their own community's assets and to address multiple needs instead of compartmentalising personnel (e.g., pastors ministering to the spiritual needs, doctors treating medical concerns).
- Developing community ownership. CHE teaches people how to identify their own problems and find a way to solve them, using locally available resources.
- Preventive vs. Curative. CHE is designed to prevent diseases for individuals, families, and communities. By providing participants with knowledge concerning basic health principles and practices, it can promote optimal health within communities.

(Source: https://www.medicalambassadors.org/our-approach/che-in-details/. Accessed 19 September 2020.)

The CHE approach also guides the training of GMV medical doctors and their definition of community development. The GMV doctors, many of whom are specialists, regard their medical expertise as only one of the necessary interventions in communities that are pursuing development. They also practise a bottom-up approach to community development that involves the locals participating in training programmes, discussions, and efforts to identify problems plaguing their community. Ideally, the locals would work closely with the GMV workers to come up with viable solutions to medical, social; environmental, cultural, and spiritual problems. The GMV asserts in its purpose statement that it serves the "holistic" needs of the people in China. In other words, for the GMV, development is necessarily holistic development. And it is the spiritual dimension that the GMV volunteers are especially interested in addressing. Elaborating on the concept of CHE in an interview, a GMV doctor underscores the importance of including the spiritual dimension in achieving what she calls "complete health":

> As a medical doctor, we're basically trained to address physical, medical, organic problems, or even mental problems. And that's what they come to see us for, that's what they expect. But conceptually, philosophically, you must address *everything*. So, I do not believe in dichotomized Christianity where you have social work versus evangelism. I do believe in a *holistic* approach and that includes the spiritual side. So, whatever I do, the spiritual side must be part of it because that's part of our human nature. So, from that point of view, I cannot say that evangelism is the driving force, but a holistic approach, which is also the biblical definition of *shalom*, peace, that peace is more than just political peace, or the lack of disease. It's harmony, it's complete health, which is the *balance* between the physical, social, the spiritual, and even environmental health [emphasis added].

When invited by the County Poverty Alleviation Bureau, the GMV offered a "holistic family health programme" that involved basic health and disease prevention training, family management, character building, and environmental education. When asked what Christianity could offer to development work and community building, one male GMV respondent, in his late 40s, links Jesus's message on the "fullness of life" with the holistic approach of community development that encompasses both spiritual and material well-being:

> Christ says that, "I'm here to give you the fullness of life." What does that "fullness" mean? That fullness is, I think, material, mental, as well as spiritual. It's not just a spiritual dimension, it is also a material dimension. And if you look at societies or communities that become Christians, they become better off naturally. Because that is the way the gospel is.

Yidan was the GMV site manager based in Meigu, Sichuan province. He oversaw the organisation's "village holistic health training" and "water infrastructure project". He referred to Bryant Myers's book *Walking with the Poor: Principles and Practices of Transformational Development* in highlighting the need to pursue sustainability in community development projects so that the community's physical, social, mental, and spiritual needs were met. Echoing the dominant discourse and approaches of global development, Yidan suggested that GMV workers needed to ask themselves the following questions in relation to the outcomes of their community development work:

> Do our projects utilise local knowledge, resources and expertise, so that as much as possible, people can manage their own health care, finances or households? Do our projects go beyond increasing productivity, while also ensure the environment's life-supporting capacity? Do our projects enable people to create their own wealth? Have we enhanced physical sustainability in communities?

From the above, it is quite clear that the GMV does not subscribe to the modernist distinction between the sacred and secular in conducting their work. For its workers, just as there is no clear boundary between evangelism and community work, there is little separation between secular and religious knowledge. Feener and Scheer (2018: 4) characterise this kind of Christian approach to development as "salvationist", with a temporality that is future-oriented and an activism that extols this-worldly interventions. This could be seen in the incorporation of management and leadership research under the GMV volunteer training programme. As the GMV administrator noted, there was much affinity between the latest research on leadership training and needs of faith-based NGOs:

> Yes, there's a lot of synergy. A lot of our materials we use are from the secular world, sensible research about emotional intelligence. So even though Daniel Goleman [the bestselling author of *Emotional Intelligence*] is an evolutionist,

the research that he does, on how people behave, how leaders affect things, is very useful for us. So, we do *crossover* quite a lot. Maybe 20–30 years ago, we would get some pushback from Christians who feel that, if I'm a Christian, I don't want anything to do with this secular stuff. But now very rarely. I think there's an understanding that universal truths are universal. There's more openness to accepting truths from different sources.

Ideological disguise

As we have defined it, ideological disguise refers to the efforts undertaken by social groups to tactically de-emphasise or "hide" their foundational ideologies in public engagements, to attain long-term strategic goals. For the GMV respondents, their involvement in community development is ultimately based on their deeply held religious ethics and commitment to the less fortunate who may also be open to evangelism. For the local government, the need to cultivate skills in areas such as leadership, business, and social services stems from its concerns over political legitimacy, socio-economic development, and nation building. Its ideological disguise involves downplaying the fact that the GMV is a Christian organisation whose members are primarily motivated by Christian values and hold the goal to gain converts in China. Both the GMV and the government authorities may be motivated by different ultimate values, but their overlapping engagement with a new paradigm of development—one that emphasises community participation and holistic development—has allowed them to participate in ideological disguise in the pursuit of a social sacred, i.e. holistic development. An organisation like the GMV would not have been able to operate at the height of Maoism in an earlier period, when the paradigm of holistic development was not promoted. And the Chinese government, due to its political framing, would have considered the GMV's work as a tool of Western imperialism.

In recent years, an important way for religious NGOs to legitimise their development efforts in China is to emphasise their "professionalism". For example, of five "core values" that guide GMV's work, one is professionalism. Due to the political sensitivity of religion, especially relating to Christianity and the presence of foreign missionaries, GMV workers often try to convince the government that they are not there to preach the gospel. If the workers avoid proselytising openly, adhere to existing rules and regulations, and demonstrate "professionalism", they are likely to encounter fewer government obstructions to their work. As one interviewee puts it, "when we work with the government, this is exactly what we say, we are here as professionals, but we don't hide the fact that we are Christians". Zhiyong was one of the early full-time workers when he first arrived in China in the early 1990s. The memories among the locals about the democracy movement and the Tiananmen incident in 1989 were still fresh in their minds. The Chinese government was still relatively unfamiliar with the work of NGOs, and was especially suspicious of foreign groups. According the Zhiyong, it was not possible to engage in community development as a "traditional missionary". Gaining the trust of the local government was a huge challenge. His team had to convince the authorities of their "professionalism":

> At that time, it is quite difficult to work in China, because the Chinese government was still not used to the idea of NGOs working in China. But China was classified [by the GMV] as a "creative access nation". You cannot go in there as a full-fledged missionary, so you must have a *professional* platform to go in, and be sensitive. Otherwise, you will jeopardise the whole work if you become too high profile, you may not get visa renewal. So, you must not go in with the pre-conception or the mindset that I'm going there to preach the gospel, no, not the traditional way. [Emphasis added]

Wenqing, one of our respondents who was an English-language teacher, was another pioneer volunteer in Sichuan. She shared that when she first arrived, the trust between the GMV and the local government took some time to be established. Again, an important way to establish trust was to be "professional":

> The trust took a while to be established. The initial part, at least for the English teaching programme, when they wanted our services, you could see that they struggled with the trust issues, like how much to trust us, and what we were doing. But in the initial stage that we sent in very well-qualified experts, so the *trust in the professional work can be established*. [Emphasis added]

Professionalism is increasingly couched in the terms of offering "value-add" for improvement and development; leadership, and entrepreneurship. As noted by Meihui, the GMV administrator we interviewed, the "value-add" also consisted of professional medical expertise:

> So, the value that we add now is mostly medical expertise, so we still have a very successful niche in sending specialists. The other thing of course is we give value because it's all *free*. Because it's all run by volunteers, all these people who pay their own way, use their own leave, and they see it as *service*. And then, of course, this means that the recipients also get it for free. Top notch expertise from top hospitals. And also, our doctors train them. So, we don't just go and do things for them, but we train their doctors and they like that.

From what most GMV workers tell us, for them there is no contradiction between being religious and being professional. Their primary motivation to engage in community development work in China derives from deeply held religious beliefs to spread God's love and the gospel through improving the lives of the disadvantaged. The most appropriate method is to bring much needed professional skills and expertise to the poorer and disadvantaged communities. As Tom, one of our respondents who was the architect, elaborated:

> I go in as a professional and I think that was my professional duty. And now the gospel, how I live it, is how the people see me do my work, how they

> see my life, how do I communicate with people. And then they become curious, "Why are you so different?" That's when I shared my testimony, why I am different. I said I had bad times, bad things, and bad habits, but when I become a Christian, my life changed. The way I treat people changed, the way I treat my children, my wife. They begin to ask questions, and they will ask, "Can you tell us a bit more?" To share with you a bit more, we must introduce the Bible to you. But we know that we shouldn't give the Bible to them because we are not supposed to.

Koehrsen and Heusen (2019) has observed that FBOs are characterised by their ability to cross boundaries and move across established lines. The GMV deliberately crosses and blur the boundaries between the sacred and secular. First, the Christian professionals working with the GMV do not believe that there is a sacred–secular divide when it comes to professional work. They considered that their work is sacred in as far as they are serving the impoverished community in keeping with the teachings of the Bible and practising incarnational ministry. Whether their work takes place in the "secular" and communist context or digital space does not change the sacredness of their Christian work. In other words, while the sacredness of the work of the clergy, namely, the priest, vicar, pastors, and so on, may be positioned in the sacredness of a church, the spiritual value of the Christian developmental workers is placated in their Christian belief and values system with which they conduct their professional work. Such sacredness therefore transcends physical and digital spaces. In addition, the GMV workers maintain the spiritual value of their work by starting and ending their meetings with prayers. Prayer meetings were also held on a monthly basis where returned volunteers share about their work in China, followed by prayers for the Chinese people, their needs, and the needs of the GMV.

On the other hand, the local governments and local communities, though not motivated by the same religious ideals, usually frame the professional help given by FBOs, like the GMV, as non-religious interventions in local social and economic development. Over the years, political leaders and policymakers in different national societies have come to embrace certain tenets of the new development paradigm. Highly pertinent to our global field framework is the fact that China's efforts in poverty reduction have relied heavily on foreign funds and involved participation of international groups. At the discursive level, China has also explicitly stated that rights to subsistence and development are basic human rights.

China's development-oriented poverty reduction programme is supported by both local and foreign efforts. It practises what the government calls "advanced concepts and methods" (e.g. participatory poverty reduction; small-sum loans; project appraisal and management, and poverty monitoring and evaluation). China has welcomed financial and technical aids from institutions such as the World Bank, the UNDP, the Asian Development Bank, and non-governmental aid organisations from other countries. According to State Council estimates, in a decade to 2010 foreign funds targeted at poverty reduction in China reached a total of US$1.4 billion, supporting around 110 foreign-funded projects in more than 300 counties in central and western China. (*White Paper on New Progress in Development-oriented Poverty Reduction Program for Rural China*). In sum, central and local state agencies, and a rising number of civic groups, have been working with international donor agencies and secular and faith-based international NGOs, to engage in community development (*shequ jianshe*) (Heberer 2009; Park and Wang 2010; Chen, Fung and Hung 2017; Shepherd 2017).

In official discourse in China, we see, for example, Ye Xiaowen, former Director-General of the State Administration of Religious Affairs, saying, "I believe, all that is true, good and beautiful are connected; be they religious or secular in form and be they be measured by the values of the East or West" (Ye 2006: 17). Cao Shengjie, former leader of the state-affiliated China Christian Council, articulates how Christian social ethical concerns are in close alignment with the goals of the government and the society at large:

> According to Romans 13:1–5, we Christians should obey the authority that rewards the good deed but punishes the wrongdoing, and to respect each other's belief and co-operate for the common good. In God's eyes, no human institution is perfect. What we can do is to support the good and resist the evil. We respect each other's different beliefs, and can still co-operate for common good … In recent years, our government advocates the building up of a "harmonious socialist society". The context of a harmonious society includes democracy and legal system, fairness and justice, credibility and friendliness, vitality, stability and order, and concord between human and nature. *These aspirations are in line with Christian social ethical concerns.*
>
> (Cao 2006, 150–151, my italics)

In practice, this means that the official Chinese church would highlight the importance of social ethics and encourage Chinese Christians to set examples in society "through living out the image of Christ" (Cao 2006: 154). Furthermore, the church would enhance its social service programmes in areas such as care for the elderly, the sick and the disabled, early childhood education, and humanitarian assistance.

A State Council White Paper, *The Right to Development: China's Philosophy, Practice and Contribution*, elaborates on the concept of balanced and comprehensive development, to include economic development, political development, cultural progress, social development, environment-friendly development, and common development. Below are excerpts of the documents (note especially the references to the United Nations, international community, and prevailing global norms and approaches to development):

> On the 30th anniversary of the publication of the "Declaration on the Right to Development by the United Nations," China, dedicated to advocating,

> practicing and promoting the right to development, is willing to join the *international community* to share its philosophy and experience in this regard and to boost sound development of *global* human rights.
>
> China will continue to work with the *international community*, strengthen cooperation, promote exchanges of experience, and make its due contribution to further increase the level of development of all peoples of the world and *build a community* with shared future for mankind.
>
> Equal access to development opportunities and development benefits are the *ideals of human society* wherein each and every citizen can achieve *well-rounded development* and enjoy full right to development.
>
> Safeguarding the right to development is the precondition for realizing economic, cultural, social and environmental rights, and obtaining civil and political rights. China appreciates the articulation in the UN's "Declaration on the Right to Development" … [italics added]

While China's official pronouncements and policies on development practice and goals seem to be aligned with the new global development paradigm, we are not suggesting here that the Chinese government and religious NGOs are in complete agreement with one another. Individuals and groups on each side may have their own political or religious agenda, and are motivated by very different ultimate values. The ruling Chinese Communist Party may be motivated by the desire to maintain its commanding heights in shaping social, political, economic, and cultural affairs within China (Shue 2011; Teets 2014). However, the Communist Party does acknowledge, in various periods, religion's potential positive contributions to society. This is reflected in the changing religious policies of the party-state, which range from a more militant form of atheism during the Cultural Revolution to the current accommodative stance that allows religion to contribute to state-defined goals. While the Ministry of Civil Affairs aims to promote "grassroots" and "community development", in practice, many local development projects keenly acknowledge the dominance and leadership of the Communist party. For example, the State Council recently issued an important document on the "consolidating and perfecting urban and rural community management" that emphasises the incorporation of Xi Jinping's ideas and strategic vision on governance, with the party's grassroots as the firm foundation for community development (Zhang 2017). At the same time, workers and volunteers in FBOs, such as the GMV, may frame their activities ultimately in religious terms. While the Christian respondents acknowledge the transcendental origin of their religious ideals and beliefs, their religious orientation is primarily this-worldly. As Jennifer, the veteran GMV worker and one-time English teacher in Sichuan province, reflected, in her email exchange with one of us:

> The doctors and nurses, in administering medical care to the wounded and training the local medical personnel, have also become a channel for God's spiritual healing to come upon the people. The counsellors in providing post-trauma counselling to the victims of the disasters, have become God's

instrument in bringing both emotional and spiritual healing to the people. These counsellors are abiding by the promise in the bible that the Holy Spirit is the counsellor who will bring comfort to the afflicted. The GMV teachers who taught in the schools in these communities show how Jesus came to the world as the Great Teacher, and taught us about God and how to live our lives. It is the belief of these Christian missionaries that Jesus' life and nature should be shown both in their professional service and how they live their daily lives in the sense of how they treat their spouses and children as well as other people.

Conclusion

Over the last few decades, both national and global civil society groups, including religious agents, have been actively and profoundly influencing the global discourse and practice of development (Thomas 2004; Clarke 2008; Tomalin 2012). This is a discursive practice that includes conceptions of community building, holistic development, and human development. States, as representatives of national societies, have also been involved in the shaping of this new development paradigm through their participation in international forums and institutions. Any religious agent participating in development is likely to portray its aims and activities as ethical and highly positive. Using the concept of the global field, we suggest that religious contribution in development should be contextualised, or relativised, in terms of four components that make up the global field of religious development ethic: the religious agent, the national society, the global civil society, and the global discursive practice of development (see Chapter 2).

Holding the four components in tension with one another, this model acknowledges a constantly changing national and global environment wherein the ideals and practises of development have been historically evolving in the dynamic negotiations and contestations between different key institutional actors. On the one hand, religious agents have introduced the spiritual dimension to development discourse and practice. On the other hand, what is considered ethical religious contribution can evolve in response, or subject to, constant negotiation with predominant national as well as global discursive practices of development. Hence, under the global field model proposed here, what is legitimate or ethical should not be construed in absolute terms, but in terms of degree and variation, and conditioned by processes of relativisation and contestation. For example, when a religious agent, such as GMV, conducts development work in China, it conscientiously draws on the prevailing global discourses on ideals of humanitarianism and development to legitimise its activities. Sociologically and politically, religious agents' participation in development will thus be complex and ethically contentious as the four components of the global field interact dynamically with one another in multiple and mutually impactful ways.

We argue that both the religious groups like the GMV and local governments are engaging in ideological disguise. Our analysis in this chapter has demonstrated that the emphasis on community building, harnessing of local and foreign resources, empowering of the grassroots, and holistic development has created an important discursive space that brings together religious NGOs (such as the GMV), local communities, and local government in China to collaborate to achieve development goals. At the same time, national societies, such as China, may also reference the same discourses in their policies on religious participation in development. Meanwhile, both the national societies and religious agents can be negotiating, collaborating, or contesting with other global civil society groups in efforts to formulate the appropriate measures to achieve developmental goals. Christian international NGOs like GMV must constantly evolve their values with simultaneous reference to national and international discursive practices of development. In China, their religious values must be embodied in the terminology of the Chinese values such as harmony, civic mindedness, and care for the community. Their professional community work has now to demonstrate an intentional goal of partnership with the local Chinese state officials and other professionals. In the landscape of rapidly growing wealth and professionalism of the Chinese, the GMV is even considering evolving itself into a business so they can maintain their presence and legitimacy in the Chinese society. The religious scene in China is therefore one that is marked by a constant negotiation between local and foreign Christian groups within a global context of shifting development paradigm. In this negotiation, the communication and exchange of religious and Chinese values flow in a flux and are embodied in terms and perspectives that both sides can understand.

6 Bearing fruits

Religious infusion in society

Christianity in evolving sociopolitical context

In recent years, the growth of Christianity in China, in terms of both numbers of believers and the intended influence of values in the society, took place amid intense state restrictions. The Chinese government has ventured to include the religious groups in its nation building and development efforts. To what extent will we see the presence and actions of the Chinese Christians effect social change in China? We are witnessing a period in which there is intense international pressure on China to apply the rule-of-law and ethics to their policies, which include giving freedom of religion to its people. Consequently, with these external and internal pressures, will China head towards a future in which it will consider and implement more ethical course of actions and policies? Conversely, there has also been increasing government pressure in terms of restrictions on the Chinese churches. Will we witness a greater resistance and counteractions from the Chinese Christians to proselytise to the unbelievers and increase the numbers in their Christian community through the creative channels they are using to spread their beliefs? In this final chapter, as a conclusion to our analyses presented in this book, we reiterate the need to go beyond the civil society approach to understand the role of religion in ameliorating social suffering through social engagement and changing moral and behavioural norms in China. We argue that the propagation of religion and Christianity in China can be described as a process of religious infusion. In the final part, we recapitulate our major findings in the book and their implications for deepening our understanding for the continuing development of religion in China.

Over the last decade, the Chinese government has called upon the religious groups to publicly proclaim their love for their country. They are recently beckoned by President Xi to demonstrate their resolve to help build the "China Dream". The party-state also demands religion to play an active role in the provision of the social services that it approves of. Such services consist of disaster relief; environmental protection; poverty alleviation; public infrastructure building; and medical, scientific, and cultural enterprises. All of these charitable works are encouraged by the state. Conversely, human rights protection and campaigning for political change are not condoned by the state. Furthermore, the party-state regards itself as custodian of religious groups. The latter must acknowledge the authority of the party-state in the management of religious affairs and are duty-bound to actively support the country's religious policies. Religious groups are also accountable to the authorities regarding donations they receive, and, subsequently, the proper use of these public funds. The government's injunction to Christians and other religious groups to "serve" the society takes a concrete legal form in the updated China's regulations on religion that came into effect in February 2018. One line reads:

> Religious groups are entitled to functions that include *assisting governments* at all levels in the implementation of laws, regulations, rules and policies, protecting the legitimate rights of citizens with religious beliefs, guiding religious affairs, researching religious culture and carrying out religious education and training.
>
> (China State Council; italics added)

The government's tightening of its reins on Christianity since Xi Jinping came to power happened after two decades of huge increase in the number of Christians (especially Protestants) in the country. Between 2014 and 2016, authorities in the eastern province of Zhejiang demolished many church buildings which allegedly violated planning regulations. Subsequently, large groups of lay believers, with the support of the clergy, held public protests. They accused the officials of abusing their authority, violating their religious freedom, and unfairly targeting their freedom of religion. However, the Chinese Christians in our study generally did not advocate or participate in such open and overt opposition of the government's actions against the churches. Rather, they adopted more under-the-radar opportunities and channels to practise their religion, like creating spaces within their businesses for Christians to meet for Bible study and prayer meetings, such as in cafes, bakeries, and restaurants. While the socialist market economy has subsumed the lives of the Chinese people in contemporary China, Chinese Christians are doing Christian work in China to "make a difference" by exhibiting Christian values in their work, conduct of business, and treatment of colleagues. As we have shown in previous chapters, many of our respondents hold their values system and beliefs to be distinctively different from the rest of the society. At the same time, this group of Chinese Christians believe that they can have an influence over people around them whom they believe to have yet subscribed to their faith. This mindset obviously gives the Chinese Christians hope in circumstances which are hostile to their faith, especially in times of state persecution. It provides them the patience and strength to wait for what they perceive to be the positive transformation of the society. Our study aims to shed light on such attempts to transform the society through mainly unobtrusive ways.

Also, in recent years we see clear evidence of an emerging consensus among lay and clerical Chinese Christians (albeit occupying different institutional and theological positions) on the need for heightened Christian social engagement while maintaining different views on the appropriateness of ties with the party-state.

This will likely have a profound impact on Christianity's role for social change in China in the future. What will be the future of increasing Christian social engagement? In our discussion in Chapter 1 on the theological underpinnings and practical efforts of Protestant and Catholic social engagement, we illustrate the important continual role Christians play in China's social change in the form of offering solutions to social suffering and changing moral and behavioural norms. Nevertheless, we need to underscore the fact that this role is constantly evolving in tandem with shifts in the country's political climate even as some Christians actively seek to change the climate (Lim 2013; Wielander 2013).

It is possible that the party-state will continue to limit Christianity's social influence even as the number of believers continues to rise. Some local government officials may also welcome the contributions of Christian organisations in the areas of social welfare provision and humanitarian assistance. One thing is clear: China's Communist leaders may accommodate Christianity at times, but will not tolerate any hint of challenge to their authority and legitimacy. In the latest development, the government has promulgated new sets of laws and regulations to further tighten its grip over religious groups in the country. As mentioned in the chapter on the work of the GMV, we describe how both local and foreign NGOs (including FBOs) now have to comply with more stringent regulations on their operations. Meanwhile, in 2020, the state updated its policies on the regulation of religious affairs by explicitly emphasising the leadership of the Communist Party. Since Xi Jinping came to power, Chinese Christians seeking greater religious freedom and public involvement are feeling the chilling effects of heightened government's surveillance and control. This can be seen in 2014 when both unofficial and official Protestant and Catholic churches in Zhejiang were targeted in a widespread government crackdown. In the last two years, the authorities have arrested prominent and critical house church leaders who had steadfastly fought for religious freedom and advocated for more civil rights.

The main approach in much of the scholarly literature in China in understanding the developments in state–religion relations is through the civil society paradigm. In the section below, we would like to revisit briefly the issue of civil society in China and put forward our views on the necessity to consider alternative approaches.

Religious infusion: rethinking religious social engagement in China

As we have discussed in Chapter 2, scholars who argue that civil society exists in China explain that the form in which it exists deviates from the liberal model found in Western democracies that forms the standard conception of civil society. It is certain that if civil society is to exist in China at all, it has to be in close interaction with an authoritarian government. For Teets (2014), the "China Model" entails a learning process whereby both civil society and local officials try to understand and learn the intentions and modus operandi of each other, and find ways to engage collaboratively in socially beneficial projects that may ultimately support the perceived legitimacy of the local governments. While local officials work with the civil society for their own agenda, they face the political risk of being challenged by emboldened civil society actors who are mobilising against governance lapses through social and protest movements. Meanwhile, civil society actors have come to grasp both the explicit and unspoken rules of engagement with the party-state. In turn, they organise themselves to provide various kinds of social services that local governments are unable to adequately provide and, subsequently, would need the contributions of civil society. In this context, civil society in China is less about democratic politics than about a highly regulated domain whereby non-governmental organisations and local officials collaborate on projects to attain public goods. At the same time, they remain ultimately under the social management of the government. At the very least, this form of civil society has facilitated more interactions and dialogue between local governments, citizens, and civic organisations.

While facing an unfavourable political climate due to the intensification of state suppression of Christian activists who are demanding social and political reforms, Chinese Christians are able to continue to be actors for social change. As the civil society in China is further restricted and curtailed, Chinese Christians are seeking to spread Christian values to change society for the better through various means. However, this may not be adequately captured in an approach that focuses on state–society relations. Therefore, in this book, we highlight the analytical usefulness of the concepts of everyday religion and unobtrusive social engagement in comprehending the actions of both the Chinese and overseas Christians in effecting their concept of social change. In the light of our methodological and substantive concerns presented in the previous chapters, we would like to recapitulate and further develop our main arguments through explicating the notion of ***religious infusion***.

In recent years, even when faced with a challenging political climate, the officially recognised religions in China—with perhaps the exception of Islam—have generally been able to continue with their legal activities that are conducted in registered religious sites such as temples, churches, and small religious "meeting places" (*ju hui dian*). As scholars of religion in China have noted, religion has generally thrived in what Gareth Fisher (2014) calls "islands of religiosity", even after decades of the party-state's violent attempts to impose a secularist rule which is aimed at stamping out religion; minimising its social influence, and converting citizens to scientism. This expression describes spaces where believers may conduct their religious activities and sustain high levels of religiosity in a relatively autonomous, supportive, and safe environment. While Fisher (2014) uses the expression primarily to describe the religious activities which are conducted in Buddhist temples, we may extend it to describe legally sanctioned religious sites as well as other venues such as homes, factories, event halls, cafes, fast-food restaurants, and online social network sites where people gather for religious activities. These official and nonofficial religious spaces may be linked and traversed by personal networks as some believers participate in, and move between, multiple "islands". Extending this metaphor, this implies that outside such islands of religiosity is a sea of "secular" social and political spaces, which are intensely monitored and tightly regulated by the authorities, where any hints of religiosity are barred by them.

We find the metaphor of "islands of religiosity" useful to examine and understand how religious spaces continue to exist and may often be sheltered from the prying eyes of the authorities. It makes us cognisant of the believers' ingenuity and commitment to practise their respective religions by crossing institutionally created spatial boundaries. The metaphor also paints a picture of a vast sea of secularity that surrounds such religious islands. It vividly portrays how an officially atheistic government may powerfully shape the boundaries of the "religious" and "secular" spaces. The metaphor also describes the overwhelming condition in which the practice of religion in China is carried out, where "moralizing discourses are...mostly confined to discrete religious environments such as temples" (Fisher 2014: 204). However, we think that the islands of religiosity metaphor draws too sharp a boundary between the "religious" and other domains of social life. It suggests a highly fragmented lived experience of believers' everyday life which may not be the case in reality. In this sense, it risks unwittingly privileging the statist-institutional perspective that differentiates social life into various distinct domains for governance and administrative purposes, when believers themselves may not experience it as they inhabit and interact within these spaces and across these domains. As we have shown in the previous chapters, for our Christian respondents religion is much more encompassing of social life than the imagery of islands of religiosity suggest. For example, unlike the Buddhists described by Fisher, they deal with and seek to resolve moral dilemmas not only in the confined religious sites such as the church. For them, social and religious concerns tend to be intertwined and encompassed within an overarching religious worldview, and demand attention and resolution in "secular" spaces such as the workplace and social media.

Therefore, instead of islands of religiosity, we propose using the notion of religious infusion to describe our Christian respondents' everyday religious experience and moralizing discourses. Think of putting a tea bag in a cup of hot water: the result is a cup of tea infusion. According to the *Merriam-Webster Dictionary*, to infuse is "to cause to be permeated with something (such as a principle or quality) that alters usually *for the better*" (italics included). Thus, religious infusion refers to the process of increasing permeation of religion and religious values into society through believers' effort of integrating religious values, worldview, and ethics into their everyday life. The notion of religious infusion should not be confused with CK Yang's (1961) "diffused religion". In his classic study of Chinese religious culture, Yang makes the distinction between institutional and diffused religion. The former refers to religion that has a socially independent institutional existence, with clear dogmas that are elaborated and systematised by authoritative groups of specialists. Christianity, Buddhism, Daoism, Islam are examples of institutional religion. Diffused religion, on the other hand, refers to religious practices whose existence and perpetuation depend on the secular institutions to which they are attached. An example of a diffused religion is ancestor worship, which is inextricably bound up with the Chinese systems of kinship structure and inheritance. Conversely, the practice of ancestor worship as a diffused religion may serve to legitimise and perpetuate the kinship structure and related interests. An important feature of diffused religion, as Yang argues, is that when the supporting secular institutions experience demise, it faces the same fate as well. However, our notion of religious infusion, unlike diffused religion, does not depend on the existence and support of any specific secular institution(s). On the one hand, it recognises the important subjective element of believers' desire in seeking to integrate religion with their everyday life. At the same time, there are various objective conditions, institutions, practices (e.g. technology, political environment, cultural practices) that believers may choose to engage with to facilitate their aim of integration.

The notion of religious infusion also allows us to inquire the extent to which believers desire or are able to integrate religion in their everyday life and spaces. Some believers or religious institutions may insist on establishing clear boundaries separating the "religious" or "sacred" from the everyday "profane" and "secular", and creating what Fisher calls "islands of religiosity". Some others, like the Christians in our study, may actively seek to integrate religion into different aspects of social life while downplaying, ignoring, negotiating, or rejecting the modernist secularist differentiation of "religion" as a separate social domain. In addition, their working out of moral dilemmas are not confined within officially demarcated religious sites. In our study, the Christians' belief and practice of religious infusion are drawn upon the biblical teaching that all of the world is created by God and His act of creation is considered as work. Subsequently, the work of Christians and the spaces of their workplace and home carry the same spiritual significance as God's work. So, for Christians to regard their surroundings as sacred and behave as such is to live in a way that is consistent with God and the teachings of the bible. As we have discussed in the earlier chapters, one important goal of such effort is ameliorating social sufferings and changing society for the better.

In our Introduction chapter, we refer to social suffering as an interpersonal ground of suffering (Kleinman, Das, and Lock 1997) that situates a person's experience of suffering in a larger web of interpersonal relations and current societal issues. The findings of our research show how our Chinese Christian respondents position themselves in a Chinese society that, in their eyes, is undergoing rapid changes; experiencing social suffering, and desperately needing a societal-wide moral reset. They hope that religious infusion will lead to positive social change through blurring or dissolving the statist institutionalisation of distinct social domains. The way these believers seek to spread Christian values and their vision of the ideal society is, therefore, a slow, unobtrusive, and long-term process that sometimes does not involve direct interaction, whether directly, or intensively, with the state. In this process of religious infusion, mundane and temporal activities like maintaining hygiene, hobbies, and work routines are ascribed a higher spiritual value. This spiritualising of mundane and temporal activities connects the Christians with the God they believe in as well as the community they live in which has yet to subscribe to their faith. The process also enables the Christians to view their existing temporal life as one continuum, connecting them with the creation of God and the eternal life that they will experience after this life on earth. Such connection to and consistency with God, the community, and their beliefs play a vital role in the sense of meaningfulness that Christians feel about their existence, work, and daily lives.

The Christians are not the only ones who are actively engaged in religious infusion in China. Similar trends can be observed in other religions in China such as Buddhism and Islam. We can apply the notion to understand the attempts by lay Buddhists in China to bring Buddhism beyond temples and monasteries and promote it as offering solutions to current social problems, thus making it more relevant to the rapidly changing society (Sun 2011; Laliberté 2012; Zhang and Ji 2018). Lay Buddhists have taken on the mantel of volunteerism and established charities to provide a wide range of social services. Some have organised classes in homes and business sites that teach Buddhist studies classes for the faithful and non-Buddhists. In urban areas, "Boss Buddhists" have sought to demonstrate compatibility of Buddhist ethics and business culture while increasing their engagement with the society. Influenced by the controversial Taiwanese Buddhist master Jingkong, some lay Buddhists in China have made use of the discourse of "traditional culture" to organise activities and classes to teach filial piety and respect for teachers as a way of establishing Buddhism's social importance. As Zhang and Ji (2018: 30–31) explain,

> This discourse did not end with religious doctrines or individual self-cultivation, but also contained a transformation plan for social well-being by cultivating 'saints' through the education of *Disciples Regulations* [*dizi gui*], hence solving social problems and natural disasters by renewing morality.

In this book, we have examined three ways by which believers strive to infuse Christianity into society: intercontextuality on social media, the discourse of service in work and the workplace; and ideological disguise in community development.

Intercontextuality

As discussed in Chapter 3, the rise of Web 2.0 and the pervasiveness of mobile internet have had a profound and lasting impact on how religion is practised in China. In particular, the ubiquity of social media usage, in numerous personal, commercial, and official interactions, can be conceptualised as a form of popular culture in which people are increasingly able to exercise greater agency. This takes the forms of making choices that are oriented to their own needs and interests, reconstituting social relations, and, at times, challenging all sorts of authorities. Chinese Muslim netizens have made use of the widespread availability of Internet and social media to go beyond the state-based framework by linking up with Chinese-speaking Muslims in the so-called "Greater China region"

(大中华地区) and strengthening religious solidarity with the Muslim world (Ho 2017: 189). At the same time, some Chinese Muslims have increased efforts to promote awareness of Islam among non-Muslims in China through the internet and social media. They did this even as the state enhanced its surveillance and control of the online spaces to prevent "cyber-terrorism" and "cyber-separatism". For example, the website of Beijing-based China Muslim Youth Club shows intercontextuality in their communication about their faith. They also engaged in religious infusion by emphasising the compatibility of Islam in different aspects of social life:

> By holding together many outstanding young people of (either) Muslims or non-Muslims, we make an integral virtual platform to all the netizens for *social life, spiritual life, literature, charity, entertainment, dating, chatting, and gathering activities*, therefore forming a concrete and harmonious social relationship on the internet.
>
> (cited in Ho 2017:192, italics added)

In her study of how members of Tzu Chi in China use WeChat, Huang (2017) refers to online social media space as a "third space". It straddles both online and offline environment, and has some degree of autonomy from state regulations and institutional religious authorities. As such, the social media third space is where religious innovations and experimentations may occur since it allows religious practitioners some degree of freedom from the controls of both religious and secular authorities. This may result in the emergence of new religious communities which revolves around charismatic figures and their followers, who constitute as "friends" or "groups". As for our argument about religious infusion, the WeChat social media is a discursive space that enables intercontextual linking of seemingly "religious" and "non-religious" topics, such as construing environmentalism in the framework of Buddhist ethics.

As in the cases of Islam and Buddhism cited above, social media usage for religious purposes is becoming ubiquitous; more varied and sophisticated among Chinese Christians. This means that the boundaries that define Christian groupings take on a more fluid and shifting nature. Hence, we observed that the Chinese Christians' praying and meditations on the Bible were often interwoven with discourses on their professional work; global news events; socialising; commentaries of daily happenings, and other seemingly mundane matters. It is true that in the daily use of social media like WeChat to make online payments, play games, read the news, share articles, offer comments on personal and social issues, etc., religious believers often do not explicitly make reference to religion or seek meaning in a religious frame. But this is precisely our point: the ubiquity of social media usage can be seen as a form of popular culture that creates a space for intercontextualisation of communication of the different spheres of the believers' life. This not only enables Chinese Christians (and believers of other faiths) to infuse religion with other seemingly "secular" issues when they deem fit. Hence, this potentially spreads religious messages throughout their social media networks. At the same time, the social media space paradoxically conceals religion via intercontextuality and makes it less explicit. This is different in both legal and illegal religious sites where religion is prominently defined by the very state institutions that wish to regulate it.

In mobile social media, the communication of religious practices like prayer, preaching, and worship singing takes place in the same media space as communication of members' daily activities, such as cooking, eating, studying, going on retreats, and moving to a new house. Christian users are motivated (but not only) by religious beliefs and principles to participate in online groups and discussion, thereby cultivating social ties which are supported by religious networks. We have argued that this can be understood with reference to the Christian notion of community as a fellowship. Chinese Christians experience the need to form a community among themselves on social media, so that their presence can influence the outer society with their Christian values. As we have shown, the features of media mixing and intercontextuality on social media allow Christian users to merge both the state-institutionalised "secular" and "religious" domains, and demonstrate how spiritual values are relevant to everyday mundane activities. Intercontextuality thus enables Chinese Christian users to communicate regularly about their daily routines and Christian values, which allows them to align their Christian concerns with wider societal issues. It also takes place in the workplace where Christians apply their values to their working behaviour and performance. This also provides an easily accessible and utilisable means for Chinese Christians to introduce their religion to the non-believers without being overtly evangelistic. In addition, it enables the Chinese Christians to fulfil what they believe to be their biblical mandate to influence society positively, which accumulatively, over time, could achieve the social change they desire.

Discourse of service

Another way through which religious infusion may occur is via the workplace. Again, our approach differs from that commonly found in existing scholarship that examines state–society relations and civil society. By contrast, we explore how Chinese Christians seek to change society in an arena that is not usually considered part of civil society and does not directly involve interacting with the state. In the workplace, Chinese Christians find themselves having to fend off the undesirable values and practices of their non-Christian bosses and colleagues, while attempting to influence the latter with their Christian values. Christians hold onto a vision of an ideal society which is guided by Christian values and principles. In an environment that is contrary, and even antagonistic, to their values, Christians construct a community among themselves, in terms of both face-to-face and virtual community. In doing so, they are able to sustain their beliefs and influence their non-believing friends simultaneously. As we have argued, evangelical Protestant employees tend to view the society as experiencing a moral decline. This view, in turn, reinforces their sense of being different and legitimises their efforts in changing society through influencing their colleagues and changing the workplace culture. Our respondents rationalise this effort in terms of work as a form of "service" to God, colleagues, and society. By attributing spiritual significance to their work and attempting to infuse religion into workplace culture, these Christians strive towards the ideal of expressing their faith more holistically in society. This, in turn, reinforces the religious values that form the basis of their ethical system and enables them to spread these values in society. In addition, these Christians believe that since their God created the world, all of creation belong to Him. The world was corrupted because of sin. Therefore, for them to live lives which are consistent to how God wants them to live and which are consistent to the teachings of the Bible is to reclaim this world for God, and one way in which they can accomplish this is in the workplaces.

But there are challenges that Christians face in their endeavour to accomplish these moralistic changes in their environment. Chinese Christian employees' merging of religion, work, and other aspects of their daily life happens in a sociopolitical context where Christians still constitute a small religious minority, and where Christianity can still be deemed a highly sensitive cultural and political issue by many believers and non-believers alike. Unlike the Christian entrepreneurs or Wenzhou's "Boss Christians", the Christian employees we interviewed do not enjoy the relative freedom and authority to openly express their faith in the workplace. Neither are they able to demand their secular firms or appeal to the country's laws to support their faith–work integration. These Christian professionals are not engaging in "political merit-making" (Weller et al. 2017) by cultivating favourable ties with party-state officials for their social engagement. Rather, they are both aware and wary of the wider sociopolitical context as they seek to practise religion in their everyday life in a more encompassing manner. In an authoritarian political context whereby civil society activism is curtailed, the workplace can provide an alternative venue for Christian employees to engage in religious transformation of society, albeit in less obtrusive and more subtle ways, outside the direct monitoring of the authorities.

Some of our respondents discursively construct a boundary between themselves and non-Christians in the workplace. They consider themselves as more motivated, understanding, having a more positive attitude toward work, which is less corruptible. This discursive self-othering is double-edged. On the one hand, it enables the Christians to construct a distinctive workplace and social identity, one that is framed in religious terms. On the other hand, this self-othering may result in them being negatively seen by non-Christian colleagues as belonging to a "different kind" (*linglei*). This can potentially accentuate the social gulf and tension that may already exist between Christian and non-Christian employees. While Christian employees may strive to be role models, many are also aware of the need to be careful when expressing and propagating their faith in the workplace. Overall, as Chinese Christians seek to infuse religion in society through the workplace, they constantly experience a tension between the desire to express their faith openly and the need to sometimes avoid explicit religious expressions. This leads them to think that it is their positive behaviour and attitude—which may differ from many people around them—which will cause others to notice and wonder why they are different. Therefore, this is a more covert and subtle influence on society which also shapes their view of their contributions and impact on society.

In sum, our respondents avoid the overt mobilisation and activism in their attempts to forge a better, more ethical, and more Christian society. Their perception and experience of moral decline and social ills in society motivate them to seek moral and social transformation, not by open advocacy through civil society activism, but through influencing their colleagues and workplace culture. The workplace is experienced as a microcosm of the wider society. It is an arena where many social problems may manifest and where Christian ethics should, therefore, be promulgated. Many respondents consider their work a means for social transformation viewed in moral terms. For them, the workplace is an arena where Christian evangelism, the perceived moral decline of contemporary society, and the supposed solution to the crisis are entangled, allowing for a distinct narrative and practice of Christian social engagement to emerge in China. In a word, for these Christian employees, the cultivation of personal piety and engaging in subtle proselytism in the workplace are a matter of not only saving souls but also transforming the moral fabric of society.

Ideological disguise

In April 2018, the State Administration of Foreign Experts Affairs revealed in an international conference a list of 40 most influential foreign experts in China during the 40 years of China's reform and opening-up period. Making the list is a European doctor from the GMV who had lived and worked with his family in Yunnan for 15 years. For the first eight years, Adam worked as a consultant to the anaesthetic and emergency departments of a county hospital in the Dali prefecture. During this time, he also conducted training programmes for local medical workers in neighbouring villages and taught English classes in some local schools. In 2003, in collaboration with the local health authorities, he started a "Rent a Goat" scheme as part of poverty alleviation efforts in the remote villages in mountainous areas. Poor households were able to "rent" up to five goats and return the same number after three years while keeping those born during this period for themselves. Between 2009 and 2016, Adam worked in a few hospitals in another prefecture to help establish departments of emergency medicine, obstetrics and gynaecology, anaesthetics, as well as running programmes to train medical workers. It is significant that in the Chinese media reports on Adam's work in Yunnan, he was described as a worker of an international charitable organisation (*guoji cishan jigou*). There is no mention of his Christian background and the fact that he belonged to a Christian organisation. Hence, ideologically and politically, government and party officials can continue to publicly adhere to Communist Party's official atheistic ideology and directives and government regulations on legitimate religious activities, while at the same time recognise the contributions to local development by religious NGOs, including the foreign ones such as the GMV.

In China, as examined through the case of the GMV, the discursive practice of development among both religious NGOs and the party-state allows for ideological disguise in their interactions with each other. For the officials and bureaucrats of the party-state, the practice of ideological disguise involves, first, the insistence on the "secular" or "non-religious" dimension of the work which is conducted by the religious NGOs, while choosing to downplay or publicly ignore the fact that the volunteers and workers may be religiously motivated. Community development (*shequ* or *shequn fazhan*) entails the improvement of local infrastructure, literacy, health care provisions, skills training, and other competencies and capabilities that are not ostensibly related to religious ideology and matters. We refer to these public goods as social sacred. For instance, on the occasion of the GMV's twentieth-anniversary celebrations in Chengdu, some government officials described its work as manifesting "positive energy" (*zheng nengliang*), a term often used in recent official discourses referring to positive, morally upright actions that contribute to the well-being of different aspects of society. Therefore, in the eyes of the authorities, the motivation and work of the GMV faith-based volunteers are framed in the ethos of nation building. This is a claim that GMV does not deny, though they themselves also regard that they conduct the community development work with the spiritual values which are compatible to the teachings of Jesus. This situation can be described as two intersecting circles. The portion that the circles converge is the area of ambiguity where both the Chinese authorities and faith-based volunteers may agree regarding the purposes of the latter's community development work. In so far as this area of ambiguity exists, the FBO volunteers deem that they have a window of opportunity to continue their influence in the Chinese community. As the state restrictions tighten, the FBO persists in creatively re-negotiating their work and role in the community so that they can continue their presence in the community. To the GMV workers, their presence in the community enables them to practise their incarnational role, to be present among the people so that their Christian values can be evident among the members of the community.

For religious NGOs such as the GMV, ideological disguise involves downplaying, or even publicly disavowing, the religious messages and intent in their community work as they interact with an officially atheistic government. Workers or volunteers of these groups are motivated by their religious beliefs and values. At the same time, they hope that some people in the communities may embrace their religion through their efforts. For the Christian professionals with the GMV, Christian service means they can engage their professional skills and training to help the needy, instead of having to leave their training and experiences to move into the traditional clergy roles of working in the church. This fusion of their religious beliefs and professional skills provides a powerful motivation for them in their developmental work since they believe they are now using the gifts and training that God has given them for service to God. In doing so, they are also demonstrating to the party-state that Christianity is relevant in society and not a set of "superstitious" beliefs. They believe that their work is holistic in the sense that they must transform the physical well-being, mental state, and spiritual welfare of their recipients. Their work has an element of "spiritual development" in the sense that they seek to bring the members of the community from "darkness" into the "light of truth", and, in the words of the GMV's founder, "work is an extension of one's worship to God". This means that, as individuals, the GMV volunteers do not need to antagonise over the divide between the "secular" nature of their work and their "sacred" worship. Rather, in their service, these two components of their lives are integrated. In this, their work is also "transformational development" (cf. Koehrsen and Heusen 2019) in that it transforms the community physically, morally, and spiritually. The transformative value of the Christians' developmental work therefore lies in the set of ethics that is embodied in their attitude towards their professional work and the community they serve. This set of ethics binds the Christian professionals together with common spiritual goals. It is also the bond between them and the community they serve as they seek to learn the cultures and languages of the local people.

At the same time, as the GMV workers pursue their development projects, they may resort to pragmatic convergence with the Chinese authorities who may be either wary or suspicious of religious groups working at the grassroots levels. The practice of ideological disguise is further supported when the religious NGOs make reference to currently pervasive discourses on "community" or "holistic development" which circulate in the global development industry to legitimise their work. Koehrsen and Heusen (2019) argue that Christian FBOs can be seen as "boundary agents" and "developmental entrepreneurs" as they integrate their various national and international narratives with religious and theological stances in their development work.

FBOs also realised that the developmental work market is competitive, and they strive to keep up with this by adopting the measures of commercial companies and employing specialised staff (ibid.). The GMV works hard to constantly improve their professionalism and image as a professional organisation. For example, it deploys very specialised and highly qualified medical doctors, businesspeople, and language teachers to conduct training for the Chinese of similar professions. The GMV's goal of "train-the-local professionals" enables the Chinese government officials to see that it aims to equip local professionals to help their own community, therefore giving much greater credibility and official recognition of their work. The GMV also employs qualified professional staff in their offices to plan, manage, and implement their development projects, ensuring the recruitment of highly qualified professional volunteers and training them in areas of cross-cultural work and communication, Christian work ethics, and the code of ethics in the GMV, so they can be effective in their adjustments to the local Chinese community. When the Chinese government decided to localise the charitable and developmental work of the Chinese rural communities, the GMV realised the need to transform its model of operations to be more of a commercial business so that it could secure a business visa in China.

As the case of GMV shows, religious groups may engage in ideological disguise because they are able to offer contributions in ways desired by the government and society. The local government is willing to engage in ideological disguise partly because they are aware of this, and accept the operations of such religious groups, while trying to publicly maintain its own ideological consistency of supporting secular atheism. It may be tempting to view the ideological disguise of the religious groups as showing a position of weakness. This will be far too simplistic. This is because an important reason the state representatives choose to engage in ideological disguise is that it is unable to (fully) match what the religious groups can offer to the local society, and, therefore, choose to allow these groups to operate despite ideological differences. Therefore, the ideological disguise undertaken by the Chinese authorities and religious groups like the GMV can facilitate religious infusion in society.

The three cases described above constitute Chinese Christians' attempts at unobtrusive social engagement. As can be recalled, the first type of unobtrusive social engagement is discursive politics, when our respondents strive to create a discursive space for their participation in social transformation. On the one hand, they question the stative distinction of the "religious" and the "secular" domains. On the other hand, they tend to attribute the main cause for much of the social suffering to a moral malaise that pervades contemporary society. Ultimately, the believers engage in this type of discursive politics to legitimatise their social engagement through community development, networked transmission of values on social media, and transforming the workplace culture. In addition, this helps them to fulfil the mandate stated in the Bible for Christians to engage in charitable work to help the poor and marginalised in society. In their Christian belief, Jesus came to create a *koinonia* or Christian fellowship in order that they may influence the wider community with Christian values. In this sense, Christians believe that the Kingdom of God can be actualised in the life they are living now, through their Christian community and their behaviour as well as interactions with others.

Our case studies have also demonstrated the second type of unobtrusive social engagement: "burrowing into" secular institutions. This is seen in the effort undertaken by the GMV to showcase their "professionalism" in medicine, education, social work, etc., as they engage state representatives and other societal actors in "holistic" community development projects. In the secular workplace, an important way for our respondents to exert their subtle influence is by aligning their Christian values with those of business and interpersonal relationships. They hope that these values will ultimately diffuse throughout the workplace and wider society. Our Christian respondents have also engaged in the third unobtrusive strategy to assimilate and blend their values into the community. Like many other FBOs working in multicultural, multireligious, and sometimes ideologically hostile environments, the GMV's approach to development is very much aligned with that of many other international development groups, which emphasises ideals such as holistic development, sustainability and community in their development projects across diverse countries and cultures. Crucially, this is also an approach which is favoured by many governments, ranging from liberal to authoritarian ones like China's. Such convergence of discursive practices between the GMV and the Chinese local government enables the former to pursue its work even as most of its informants frame their motivation in religious terms.

Conclusion

This book sets out to address two important questions regarding Christianity in China. First, how does Christianity continue to experience growth in an increasingly authoritarian political system that enforces strict regulations on religion? Second, how are ordinary Chinese Christians affected by social and political changes in the country, and how do they make their influence felt in the wider society? By focusing the Chinese Christians' experiences, in the mainland but also transnationally, we hope to contribute to the broader scholarship on religious social engagement, especially in current and former Communist countries that practise some forms of atheist secularism. An important factor behind the continued growth of religion and its social influence is the pervasiveness of social media communications as a form of popular culture. This leads the religious practitioners to form "portable communities" as they engage in everyday activities outside government-defined "religious" domain and legally recognised physical religious sites. Social media platforms such as WeChat, QQ, and Facebook (especially for overseas Chinese) host religious networks and interactions both translocally and transnationally, facilitating what we have termed networked transmission of religious values through features of media mixing and intercontextuality. Chinese Christians make use of such features to support one another's faith and spread Christianity to their non-Christian friends or colleagues on social media. It is precisely this "mundaneness" or "everydayness" of the practice that makes it very difficult for the authorities to surveil and manage to keep religion within designated sites. We are not claiming that our respondents always intend to spread Christian messages when using the social media or frame all activities they conduct on these platforms in religious terms. Like many other users, Chinese Christians use social media for various purposes such as entertainment, financial and commercial transactions, debates with one another, reading of the news, maintenance of contacts with friends and loved ones, etc. What we are trying to analyse and highlight in this book is how Chinese Christians may seek to imbue their social media communications with religious significance and in turn spread religious values through their online networks that may circumvent the restrictions imposed by the authorities.

Apart from the ubiquity of social media, another factor that contributes to the continued expansion of religion in the society is the domain of the workplace. The workplace tends not to be included under civil society and, hence, not subject to the same degree of government scrutiny and restrictions. Like social media, work and the workplace have the same kind of "mundaneness" that allows religion to hide its head. Again, like in the case of social media, we are not arguing that our respondents and other Chinese Christians are constantly obsessed with proselytising and changing the workplace culture. They face the same kinds of challenges and problems at the workplace as other people, the daily grinding toils, boredom, politicking, seeking recognition and advancement, etc. However, we do want to underscore the fact that for many of the Chinese Christians we interviewed, work is not just a source of livelihood. It is also a sacred task performed as a practice of piety and service to God. Furthermore, many of them regard work as an opportunity to embed religion in their everyday life, and the workplace as an arena within which religious values may be cultivated and spread to transform others. In this sense, then, work can be considered as a form of unobtrusive social engagement that is aimed at the broader moral transformation of society.

Another kind of unobtrusive religious social engagement is in the realm of community development. An important point to note is that the party-state needs religion. It needs religion both as an ideological foil for self-definition and as an important symbolic and material resource for attaining its social goals. As we have argued, China's form of atheist secularisation has granted religion its social legitimacy. For Christianity, an important area where it has gained legitimacy to participate in social change is community development. We have argued that, from a global field perspective, faith-based NGOs may intervene in the forging and attainment of the social sacred by contributing to "holistic development". We have suggested that this process can be understood through the concept of ideological disguise. Under ideological disguise, faith-based NGOs and local governments may seek to conceal or downplay their ideological differences and publicly work together to achieve the social sacred. In the foreseeable future, there is little doubt that the party-state will continue to keep a tight rein over religion. Although our primary focus in this book is Christianity, we believe that our arguments may be applied to the situation of religion in China in general. Civil society may be curtailed and religious groups will continue to face a harsh political climate. Equally, there is little doubt that, through the processes we have analysed, religion will continue to infuse into Chinese society.

References

Abend, G. 2011. Thick concepts and the moral brain. *European Journal of Sociology* 52(1): 87–125. https://www.cambridge.org/core/journals/european-journal-of-sociology-archives-europeennes-de-sociologie/article/thick-concepts-and-the-moral-brain/92B2CA9C7B184CC940BE9D9B68F6940C

Aikman, D. 2003. *Jesus in Beijing: How Christianity is transforming China and changing the global balance of power*. Washington, DC: Regnery.

Akanbi, S.O., and J. Beyers. 2017. The church as a catalyst for transformation in the society. *HTS Teologiese Studies/Theological Studies* 73(4): a4635. https://doi.org/10.4102/hts.v73i4.4635.

Ammerman, N.T., ed. 2007. *Everyday religion*. New York: Oxford University Press.

Ammerman, N.T. 2013. *Sacred stories, spiritual tribes: Finding religion in everyday life*. New York: Oxford University Press.

Anderson, A.H. 2014. Pentecostalism and charismatic movements in Asia. In *Oxford handbook of Christianity in Asia*, ed. F. Wilfred. Oxford: Oxford University Press. https://doi.org/10.1093/oxfordhb/9780199329069.013.0010.

Barton, B. 1925. *The man nobody knows: A discovery of the real Jesus*. Indianapolis, IN: Bobbs-Merrill Company.

Bautista, J., and F.K.G. Lim, eds. 2009. *Christianity and the state in Asia: Complicity and conflict*. London and New York: Routledge.

Bays, D. 2012. *A new history of Christianity in China*. Oxford: Wiley-Blackwell.

Benefiel, M. 2005. The second half of the journey: Spiritual leadership for organizational transformation. *The Leadership Quarterly* 16: 723–747.

Bloome, D., M. Beierle, M. Grigorenko, and S. Goldman. 2009. Learning over time: Uses of intercontextuality, collective memories, and classroom chronotypes in the construction of learning opportunities in a ninth-grade language arts classroom. *Language and Education* 23(4): 313–334.

Bosch, D.J. 2007. *Transforming mission: Paradigm shifts in theology of missions*. Maryknoll, NY: Orbis Books.

Bottero, W. 2004. Class identities and the identity of class. *Sociology* 38: 985–1003.

Bourdieu, P. 1987. *Distinction: A social critique of the judgement of taste*. Cambridge: Harvard University Press.

Brasher, B. 2001. *Give me that online religion*. New Brunswick, NJ: Rutgers University Press.

Campbell, H. 2005. *Exploring religious community online: We are one in the network*. New York: Peter Lang.

Campbell, H. 2010. *When religion meets new media*. London and New York: Routledge.

Cao, N. 2011. *Constructing China's Jerusalem: Christians, power and place in contemporary Wenzhou*. Stanford, CA: Stanford University Press.

Cao, N. 2013. Elite Christianity and spiritual nationalism. *Chinese Sociological Review* 45: 27–47.

Cao, S. 2006. The role of Chinese Christians in the development of China. In *Pilgrims and citizens: Christian social engagement in East Asia today*, ed. M. Poon, 147–156. Adelaide: ATF Press.

Carino, T.C. 2016. Faith-based organisations between service delivery and social change in contemporary China: The experience of Amity Foundation. *HTS Telogiese Studies/ Theological Studies* 72(4): a3504. http://dx.doi.org/10.4102/hts.v72i4.3504.

Carpenter, J.A. and K.R. den Dulk, eds. 2014. *Christianity in Chinese public life: Religion, society and the rule of law*. New York: Palgrave Macmillan.

Castells, M. 2001. *The internet galaxy*. Oxford: Oxford University Press.

Chan, K.K., and T. Yamamori. 2002. *Holistic entrepreneurs in China: A handbook on the World Trade Organization and new opportunities for Christians*. Pasadena, CA: William Carey.

Chan, S-H. 2013. Changing church-state relations in contemporary China. *Chinese Sociological Review* 45(2): 65–77.

Chan, S-H. 2016. Changing church-state relations in contemporary China: The case of Wenzhou Diocese. *International Sociology* 34(4): 1–19. http://dx.doi.org/10.1177/ 0268580916643258.

Charbonnier, J.-P. 2007. *Christians in China, A.D. 600–2000*. San Francisco, CA: Ignatius Press.

Chau, A. 2005. The politics of legitimation and the revival of popular religion in Shaanbei, North-Central China. *Modern China* 31(2): 236–278.

Chayko, M. 2008. *Portable communities: The social dynamics of online and mobile connectedness*. Albany, NY: SUNY Press.

Chen, C.-Y., and C-F. Yang. 2012. The impact of spiritual leadership on organizational citizenship behavior: A multi-sample analysis. *Journal of Business Ethics* 105: 107–114.

Chen, S., K. Fung, and S. Hung. 2017. The changing faces of community development in China: The case of Beijing. *Community Development Journal* 52(1): 38–54. https:// doi.org/10.1093/cdj/bsw045.

China Church Voices. Christian netizens react to the Ya'an earthquake. *ChinaSource*. https://www.chinasource.org/resource-library/chinese-church-voices/christian-netizens-react-to-the-yaan-earthquake (accessed 4 October 2019).

China Church Voices. See, I am coming like a thief! Blessed is the one who stays awake and is clothed, not going about naked and exposed to shame. *ChinaSource*. https://www.chinasource.org/?s=See%2C+I+am+coming+like+a+thief%21+Blessed+is+the+one+who+stays+awake+and+is+clothed%2C+not+going+about+naked+and+exposed+to+shame (accessed 1 August 2008).

Chow, A. 2018. *Chinese public theology: Generational shifts and Confucian imagination in Chinese Christianity*. Oxford: Oxford University Press.

Ci, J. 2009. The moral crisis in Post-Mao China: Prolegomenon to a philosophical analysis. *Diogenes* 221: 19–25.

Clarke, G. 2008. Faith-based organizations and international development: An overview. In *Development, civil society and faith-based organizations*, eds. G. Clarke, and M. Jennings, 17–45. Basingstoke and New York: Palgrave.

Cochran, C.E. 2014[1990]. *Religion in public and private life*. New York: Routledge.

Cohen, P. 1963. *China and Christianity.* Cambridge, MA: Harvard University Press.
Crampton, T. 2011. Social media in China: The same, but different. *China Business Review.* January 1. https://www.chinabusinessreview.com/social-media-in-china-the-same-but-different/ (accessed 2 July 2020).
Crossman, J.E. 2015. Being on the outer: The risks and benefits of spiritual self-disclosure in the Australian workplace. *Journal of Management & Organization* 21: 772–785.
Diamond, N. 1996. Christianity and the Hua Miao: Writing and power. In *Christianity in China: From eighteenth century to the present*, ed. D. Bays, 138–157. Stanford, CA: Stanford University Press.
Duchon, D., and D.A. Plowman. 2005. Nurturing the spirit at work: Impact on work unit performance. *The Leadership Quarterly* 16: 807–833.
Ellul, J. 1964. *The technological society.* New York: Vintage Books.
Eng, I., and Y.-M. Lin. 2002. Religious festivities, communal rivalry, and restructuring of authority relations in rural Chaozhou, Southeast China. *The Journal of Asian Studies* 61(4): 1259–1285.
Fällman, F. 2010. Useful opium? 'Adapted religion' and 'harmony' in contemporary China. *Journal of Contemporary China* 19(67): 949–969.
Feener, R.M., and C. Scheer. 2018. Development's mission. In *The mission of development*, eds. R.M. Feener, and C. Scheer, 1–27. Leiden: Brill.
Fernando, M. 2002. The place of self-actualisation in workplace spirituality: Evidence from Sri Lanka. *Culture and Religion* 9: 233–249.
Fisher, G. 2014. *From comrades to bodhisattvas: Moral dimensions of lay Buddhist practice in contemporary China.* Honolulu: University of Hawai'i Press.
Fisher, G. 2017. Lay Buddhists and moral activism in contemporary China. *Review of Religion and Chinese Society* 4(2): 247–270.
Fligstein, N., and D. McAdam. 2012. *A theory of fields.* New York: Oxford University Press.
Frey, C. 2008. Beruf: Luther, Weber, Agamben. *New German Critique* 35: 35–56.
Fry, L.W., L.L. Matherly, and J.-R. Quimet. 2010. The spiritual leadership balanced scorecard business model: The case of the Cordon-Bleu Tomasso Corporation. *Journal of Management, Spirituality & Religion* 7: 283–314.
Fulton, B. 2015. *China's urban Christians: A light that cannot be hidden.* Eugene, OR: Pickwick Publications.
Gao, S. 2005. *Dangdai Beijing de jidujiao yu jidujiaotu: zongjiao shehuixue ge'an yanjiu*, Hong Kong: Daofeng Shushe.
Ghumman, S., and L. Jackson. 2010. The downside of religious attire: The Muslim headscarf and expectations of obtaining employment. *Journal of Organizational Behavior* 31: 4–23.
Giacolone, R.A., and C.L. Jurkiewicz. 2003. Toward a science of workplace spirituality. In *Handbook of workplace spirituality and organizational performance*, eds. R.A. Giacolone, and C.L. Jurkewicz, 2–28. Armonk, NY: M.E. Sharpe.
González-González, M. 2018. Reconciling spirituality and workplace: Towards a balanced proposal for occupational health. *Journal of Religion and Health* 57: 349–359.
Goulet, D. 1988. Tasks and methods in development ethics. Kellog Institute Working Paper.
Gregory, R.F. 2011. *Encountering religion in the workplace: The legal rights and responsibilities of workers and employers.* Ithaca, NY: ILR Press.
Gutterman, D.S. 2018. *Prophetic politics: Christian social movements and American democracy.* Ithaca, NY: Cornell University Press.

Hall, D.D., ed. 1997. *Lived religion in America: Toward a theory of practice*. Princeton, NJ: Princeton University Press.

Han, J. 2000. *Jidu jiao yu Yunnan shaoshu minzu*. Kunming: Yunnan renmin chubanshe.

Han, R. 2018. *Contesting cyberspace in China: Online expression and authoritarian resilience*. New York: Columbia University Press.

Han, S. and M.N. Kamaludeen. 2016. *Digital culture and religion in Asia*. London and New York: Routledge.

Hanafin, J.J. 2002. Morality and the market in China: Some contemporary views. *Business Ethics Quarterly* 12: 1–18.

Harnack, A. 1961. *The mission and expansion of Christianity in the first three centuries*. New York: Harper Touchbook.

Harrell, S., ed. 1995. *Cultural encounters on China's ethnic frontiers*. Seattle: University of Washington Press.

Heberer, T. 2009. Evolvement of citizenship in urban China or authoritarian communitarianism? *Journal of Contemporary China* 18(61): 491–515. https://doi.org/10.1080/10670560903033786.

Helland, C. 2005. Online religion as lived religion: Methodological issues in the study of religious participation on the Internet. *Heidelberg Journal of Religions on the Internet* 1(1): 1–16.

Herold, D.K., and P. Marolt. 2011. *Online society in China: Creating, celebrating, and instrumentalising the online carnival*. Oxford and New York: Routledge.

Hicks, D.A. 2003. *Religion and the workplace: Pluralism, spirituality, leadership*. Cambridge: Cambridge University Press.

Hirono, M. 2008. *Civilizing missions: International religious agencies in China*. New York: Palgrave.

Hitlin, S., and S. Vaisey. 2013. The new sociology of morality. *Annual Review of Sociology* 39: 51–68.

Hjarvard, S. 2008. The mediatization of religion: A theory of the media as agents of religious change. *Northern Lights: Film & Media Studies Yearbook* 6(1): 9–26.

Hjarvard, S. 2011. The mediatisation of religion: Theorising religion, media and social change. *Culture and Religion* 12(2): 119–135.

Ho, W-Y. 2017. Digital Islam across the Greater China: Connecting virtual *ummah* to the Chinese-speaking Muslim netizens. In *Religion and media in China*, ed. S. Travagnin, 187–203. London and New York: Routledge.

Hovey, C., and E. Philips, eds. 2015. *The Cambridge companion to Christian political theology*. Cambridge: Cambridge University Press.

Hsu, C.L. 2008. Rehabilitating charity in China: The case of Project Hope and the rise of non-profit organizations. *Journal of Civil Society* 4(2): 81–96. https://doi.org/10.1080/17448680802335144.

Huang, J. 2012. *Xiangchun sheqü de xinyang, zhengzhi yu shenguo*. Hong Kong: Chung Chi College.

Huang, W. 2017. WeChat together about the Buddha: The construction of sacred space and religious community in Shanghai through social media. In *Religion and media in China*, ed. S. Travagnin, 110–128. London and New York: Routledge.

Inglehart, R., and W.E. Baker. 2000. Modernization, cultural change, and the persistence of traditional values. *American Sociological Review* 65(1): 19–51.

Jenkins, P. 2011. *The next Christendom: The coming of global Christianity*. Oxford: Oxford University Press.

Ji, Z. 2008. Secularization as religious restructuring: Statist institutionalization of Chinese Buddhism and its paradoxes. In *Chinese religiosities: Afflictions of modernity and state formation*, ed. M. Yang, 233–260. Berkeley: University of California Press.

Ji, Z. 2015. Secularization without secularism: The political-religious configuration of post-1989 China. In *Atheist secularism and its discontent*, eds. T.T.T. Ngo, and J.B. Quijada, 92–111. London: Palgrave Macmillan.

Johnson, I. 2017. Is a Buddhist group changing China? Or is China changing it? *New York Times*, 24 June.

Kamoche, K. 2012. Managing people "spiritually": A Bourdieusian critique. *Work, Employment & Society* 26: 497–513.

Kang, J. 2016. *House church Christianity in China: From rural preachers to city pastors.* New York: Palgrave Macmillan.

Kang, X., and H. Heng. 2008. Graduated controls: The state-society relationship in contemporary China. *Modern China* 34: 36–55. https://doi.org/10.1177/0097700407308138.

Katzenstein, M.F. 1990. Feminism within American institutions: Unobtrusive mobilization in the 1980s. *Signs* 16: 27–54.

Klandermans, B. 1988. The formation and mobilization of consensus. In *From structure to action: Comparing social movement research across cultures*, eds. B. Klandermans, K. Hanspeter, and S.G. Tarrow, 173–196. Greenwich: JAI Press.

Kleinman, A., V. Das, and M. Lock. 1997. *Social suffering*. Berkeley and Los Angeles: University of California Press.

Koehrsen, J., and A. Heuser, eds. 2019. *Faith based organizations in development: Discourses and practice*. London: Routledge.

Koesel, K.J. 2014. China patriotic Pentecostals. *Review of Religion and Chinese Society* 1: 131–155.

Kraus, N.C. 1993. *The community of the spirit.* Ontario: Herald Press.

Kuah-Pearce, K.E. 2014. Understanding suffering and giving compassion: The reach of socially engaged Buddhism into China. *Anthropology and Medicine* 21(1): 27–42.

Kuah-Pearce, K.E., A. Kleinman, and E. Harrison. 2014. Social suffering and the culture of compassion in a morally divided China. *Social Science and Medicine* 21(1): 1–7.

Kucinskas, J. 2014. The unobtrusive tactics of religious movements. *Sociology of Religion* 75(4): 537–550.

Laliberté, A. 2011. Contemporary issues in state-religion relations. In *Chinese religious life*, eds. D.A. Palmer, G. Shive, and P.L. Wickeri, 191–208. New York: Oxford University Press.

Laliberté, A. 2012. Buddhist charities and China's social policy: An opportunity for alternate civility? *Archives des sciences sociales des religions* 158: 95–117.

Laliberté, A., D.A. Palmer, and K. Wu. 2011. Religious philanthropy and Chinese civil society. In *Chinese religious life*, eds. D.A. Palmer, G. Shive, and P.L. Wickeri, 139–151. New York: Oxford University Press.

Lamont, M. 1992. *Money, morals and manners: The culture of the French and American upper middle class.* Chicago, IL: University of Chicago Press.

Lamont, M., and L. Thévenot. 2000. *Rethinking comparative cultural sociology.* New York: Cambridge University Press.

Lee, C., and L. Han. 2016. Faith-based organization and transnational voluntarism in China: A case study of the Malaysia Airline MH370 incident. *Voluntas* 27: 2353–2373.

Lee, K.-H., D. McCann, and M.C. Yuen. 2012. *Christ and business culture.* Hong Kong: Centre for the Study of Religion and Chinese Society.

Leung, B. 2005. China's religious freedom policy: The art of managing religious activity. *The China Quarterly* 184: 894–913.

Leung, P.Y.S. 2007. Christian higher education in China. In *Christian responses to Asian challenges*, eds. P. Leung, and P. Ng, 23–52. Hong Kong: Chung Chi College.

Lian, X. 2010. *Redeemed by fire: The rise of popular Christianity in modern China*. New Haven, CT: Yale University Press.

Liang, J. 1999. *Gaige kaifang yilai de zhongguo noncun jiaohui*. Hong Kong: Alliance Bible Seminary.

Liang, Y. 2014. Morality, gift and market: Communal temple restoration in Southwest China. *The Asia Pacific Journal of Anthropology* 15: 414–432.

Liao, Y. 2011. *God is red: The secret history of how Christianity survived and flourished in communist China*. New York: Harper Collins.

Lim, D.S. 2013. Mission as transformation: Holistic, ecumenical, and contextual. In *Reformed mission in an age of World Christianity*, ed. S.J. Roels, 57–72. Grand Rapids, MI: Calvin.

Lim, F.K.G. 2009a. Negotiating "foreignness", localizing faith: Tibetan Catholicism in the Yunnan-Tibet borderlands. In *Christianity and the state in contemporary Asia: Complicity and conflict*, eds. J. Bautista, and F.K.G. Lim, 79–96. London: Routledge.

Lim, F.K.G. 2009b. Charismatic technology. In *Mediating piety: Technology and religion in contemporary Asia*, ed. F.K.G. Lim, 1–24. Leiden and Boston, MA: Brill.

Lim, F.K.G., ed. 2013. *Christianity in contemporary China: Socio-cultural perspectives*. London: Routledge.

Lim, F.K.G. 2020. Religion and development ethics in global perspective: A case study of a foreign Christian NGO in China. *Journal of Contemporary Religion* 35(1): 13–30. https://doi.org/10.1080/13537903.2020.1695793.

Lin, Z. 1993. *Jidujiao yu zhongguo lunji*. Taipei: Yuzhouguang chubanshe.

Liu, J. 2008. *Zhongguo jidujiao xiangcun jianshe yundong yanjiu*. Tianjin: Tianjin renmin chubanshe.

Liu, S.-D. 2006. China's popular nationalism on the internet. Report on the 2005 anti-Japanese network struggles. *Inter-Asia Cultural Studies* 7: 1.

Lohfink, G. 1984. *Jesus and community: The social dimension of Christian faith*. Minneapolis, MN: Augsburg Fortress Publishing.

Lozada, E.P., Jr. 2001. *God Aboveground: Catholic Church, postsocialist state, and transnational processes in a Chinese village*. Stanford, CA: Stanford University Press.

Lu, J., and Y. Qiu. 2013. Microblogging and social change in Asia. *Asian Perspective* 37(3): 305–331.

Lundby, K., ed. 2013. *Religion across media: From early antiquity to late modernity*. New York: Peter Lang.

Lukes, S. 2008. *Moral relativism*. New York: Picador.

Lunn, J. 2009. The role of religion, spirituality and faith in development: A critical theory approach. *Third World Quarterly* 30: 937–951. https://doi.org/10.1080/01436590902959180.

Luova, O. 2017. Charity paradigm change in contemporary China: From anti-socialist activity to civic duty. *China Information* 31(2): 137–154. https://doi.org/10.1177/0920203X17715759.

Lutz, J.G. 1971. *China and the Christian colleges, 1850–1950*. Ithaca, NY: Cornell University Press.

Ma, L., and J. Li. 2014. Remaking the civic space: The rise of unregistered protestantism and civic engagement in urban China. In *Christianity in Chinese public life: Religion, society and the rule of law*, eds. J.A. Carpenter, K. den Dulk, and K.R. den Dulk, 11–28. New York: Palgrave Macmillan.

Ma, L., and J. Li. 2018. *Surviving the state, remaking the church: A sociological portrait of Christians in Mainland China*. Eugene, OR: Pickwick Publications.

Ma, Q. 2006. *Non-Governmental organizations in contemporary China*. London and New York: Routledge.

MacCulloch, D. 2010. *A history of Christianity*. London: Penguin Books.

Madsen, R. 1998. *China's Catholics: Tragedy and hope in an emerging civil society*. Berkeley: University of California Press.

Madsen, R. 2010. The upsurge of religion in China. *Journal of Democracy* 21(4): 58–71.

Marolt, P. 2011. Grassroots agency in a civil sphere? Rethinking internet control in China. In *Online society in China: Creating, celebrating and instrumentalising the online carnival*, eds. D.K. Herold, and P. Marolt, 53–68. London and New York: Routledge.

Martin, D. 2002. *Pentecostalism: The world their parish*. Oxford: Blackwell Publishers.

McCarthy, S.K. 2013. Serving society, repurposing the State: Religious charity and resistance in China. *China Journal* 70: 48–72. DOI: 10.1086/671330.

McGuire, M.B. 2008. *Lived religion: Faith and practice in everyday life*. Oxford: Oxford University Press.

Merriam-Webster. Infusing. https://www.merriam-webster.com/dictionary/infusing (accessed 19 April 2020).

Miller, D.W. 2007. *God at work: The history and promise of the faith at work movement*. New York: Oxford University Press.

Mitroff, I.I., and E.A. Denton. 1999. *A spiritual audit of corporate America: A hard look at spirituality, religion, and values in the workplace*. San Francisco, CA: Jossey-Bass.

Morris, R. 1986. *Rethinking social welfare: Why care for the stranger?* New York: Longman.

Mythen, G., S. Walklate, and F. Khan. 2009. I'm a Muslim, but I'm not a terrorist: Victimization, risk identities and the performance of safety. *British Journal of Criminology* 49: 736–754.

Narayanan, Y. 2013. Religion and sustainable development: Analyzing the connections. *Sustainable Development* 21: 131–139. https://doi.org/10.1002/sd.1557.

Negro, G. 2017. *The Internet in China: From infrastructure to a nascent civil society*. Basingstoke: Palgrave Macmillan.

Ng, P.T.M., F. Tao, X. Zhao, and X. Liu. 2005. *Shengshan jiaoxia de shizijia*. Hong Kong: Institute of Sino-Christian Studies.

Ngo, T.T.T., and J.B. Quijada, eds. 2015. *Atheist secularism and its discontent*. London: Palgrave Macmillan.

Osburg, J. 2013. *Anxious wealth: Money and morality among China's new rich*. Stanford, CA: Stanford University Press.

Park, A., and S. Wang. 2010. Community-based development and poverty alleviation: An evaluation of China's poor village investment program. *Journal of Public Economics* 94(9): 790–799. https://doi.org/10.1016/j.jpubeco.2010.06.005.

Parsons, T., and E.A. Shils, eds. 1951. *Towards a general theory of action*. Cambridge, MA: Harvard University Press.

Pew Research Center. 2012. *The global religious landscape*. Washington, DC: Pew Research Center.

Pillay, J. 2017. The church as a transformation and change agent. *HTS Teologiese Studies/Theological Studies* 73(3): 4352. https://doi.org/10.4102/hts.v73i3.4352 (accessed 12 June 2020).

Poe, M.A. 2012. Good news for the poor: Christian influences on social welfare. In *Christianity and social work*, eds. T.L. Scales, and M.S. Kelly, 9–22. Botsford, CT: North American Association of Christians in Social Work.

Poon, M., ed. 2006. *Pilgrims and citizens: Christian social engagement in East Asia today*. Adelaide: ATP Press.

Qin, D. 2019. The evolution of evangelical socio-political approaches in contemporary China (1980s–2010s). Ph.D. diss., University of Edinburgh.

Rees, J. 2013. Religion and international financial institutions. In *Handbook of research on development and religion*, ed. M. Clarke, 268–285. Northhampton, MA: E. Elgar.

Robert, A., and S.J. White. 2007. The media, culture and religion perspective. *Communication Research Trends* 26: 1–24.

Robertson, R. 1992. *Globalization: Social theory and global culture*. Thousand Oaks, CA: Sage.

Rodney, S., and X. Wang. 2011. *A star in the East: The rise of Christianity in China*. West Conshohocken, PA: Templeton Press.

Sass, J.S. 2000. Characterizing organizational spirituality: An organizational communication culture approach. *Communication Studies* 51: 195–207.

Scheitle, C.P., and E.H. Ecklund. 2017. Examining the effects of exposure to religion in the workplace on perceptions of religious discrimination. *Review of Religious Research* 59(1): 1–20.

Schielke, S., and L. Debevec, eds. 2012. *Ordinary lives and grand schemes: An anthropology of everyday religion*. Oxford: Berghahn Books.

Shepherd, R.J. 2017. UNESCO's tangled web of preservation: Community, heritage and development in China. *Journal of Contemporary Asia* 47(4): 557–574. https://doi.org/10.1080/00472336.2017.1296174.

Shue, V. 2011. The political economy of compassion: China's "Charity Supermarket" saga. *Journal of Contemporary China* 20(72): 751–772. https://doi.org/10.1080/10670564.2011.604493.

Sloane-White, P. 2011. Working in the Islamic economy: Sharia-ization and the Malaysian workplace. *Sojourn* 26: 304–334.

Smith, C. 2003. *Moral, believing animals*. New York: Oxford University Press.

Smith, C.T. 1985. *Chinese Christians: Elites, middlemen and the Church in China*. Hong Kong: Oxford University Press.

Smith, J. 1987. Benevolent societies: The reshaping of charity during the late Ming and early Ch'ing. *Journal of Asian Studies* 46: 309–337. https://doi.org/10.2307/2056017.

Smith, J. 2009. *The art of doing good: Charity in late Ming China*. Berkeley: University of California Press.

Spates, J.L. 1983. The sociology of values. *Annual Review of Sociology* 9: 27–49.

Spence, J.D. 1984. *The memory palace of Matteo Ricci*. New York: Viking Penguin.

Stansbury, J. 2015. Moral imagination as a reformational influence in the workplace. *Journal of Markets and Morality* 18: 21–41.

Starr, C. 2015. Wang Yi and the 95 theses of the Chinese reformed church. *Religions* 2016(7): 142. https://doi.org/10.3390/rel7120142.

State Council Information Office of the People's Republic of China. The right to development: China's philosophy, practice and contribution. http://www.scio.gov.cn/zfbps/32832/Document/1534707/1534707.htm (accessed 1 July 2020).

State Council of the People's Republic of China. New progress in development-oriented poverty reduction program for rural China. http://english.www.gov.cn/archive/white_paper/2014/09/09/content_281474986284672.htm (accessed 19 March 2019).

Sun, H. 2010. *Internet policy in China: A field study of Internet cafés*. Lanham, MD: Lexington Books.

Sun, Y. 2011. The Chinese Buddhist ecology in post-Mao China: Contours, types and dynamics. *Social Compass* 58(4): 498–510.

Sun, Y. 2017. The rise of protestantism in post-Mao China: State and religion in historical perspective. *American Journal of Sociology* 122(6): 1664–1725.

Tai, Z. 2006. *The internet in China: Cyberspace and civil society*. New York and London: Routledge.

Tan, C.B. 2012. *Shantang*: Charitable temples in China, Singapore, and Malaysia. *Asian Ethnology* 71: 75–107.

Teets, J.C. 2014. *Civil society under authoritarianism: The China model*. New York: Cambridge University Press.

Teng, S.Y. 1971. *The Taiping rebellion and the western powers*. Oxford: Oxford University Press.

Thomas, S.M. 2004. Faith and foreign aid: How the World Bank got religion. *Review of Faith and International Affairs* 2: 21–30. https://doi.org/10.1080/15435725.2004.9523180.

T'ien, J-K. 1993. *Peaks of faith: Protestant missionaries in revolutionary China*. Leiden: E.J. Brill.

Tomalin, E. 2012. Thinking about faith-based organisations in development: Where have we got to and what next? *Development in Practice* 22: 689–703. https://doi.org/10.1080/09614524.2012.686600.

Tong, J. 2012. *Overseas Chinese Christian entrepreneurs in modern China*. London: Anthem Press.

Tong, J., and F. Yang. 2016. Trust at work: A study on faith and trust of Protestant entrepreneurs in China. *Religions* 7(12): 136. https://doi.org/10.3390/rel7120136.

Travagnin, S., ed. 2017. *Religion and media in China*. London: Routledge.

Uhalley, S., and X. Wu, eds. 2001. *China and Christianity: Burdened past, hopeful future*. Armonk, NY: M.E. Sharpe.

UNDP. 1994. Human development report. http://hdr.undp.org/en/content/human-development-report-1994 (accessed 23 November 2018).

Vala, C. 2018. *The politics of Protestant churches and the party-state in China: God above party?* New York: Routledge.

Vala, C., and J. Huang. 2017. Three high-profile protestant microbloggers in contemporary China: Expanding public discourse or burrowing into religious niches on Weibo? In *Religion and media in China*, ed. S. Travagnin, 167–186. New York and London: Routledge.

Wallace, R., and S. Bruce. 1995. Secularization: The orthodox model. In *The sociology of religion*, vol. 1, ed. S. Bruce, 8–30. Aldershot: Elgar.

Wang, A. 2001. The nature and purpose of theological reconstruction in the Chinese Church. *Chinese Theological Review* 15: 19–26.

Wang, L. 2008. *Meiguo chuanjiaoshi yu wanqing zhongguo xiandaihua*. Tianjin: Renmin chubanshe.

Warren, R. 2014. *The purpose driven life*. Philadelphia, PA: Running Press.

Weller, R.P. 2006. Religions and philanthropies in Chinese societies. *Society* 44: 42–49.

Weller, R.P., C.J. Huang, K. Wu, and L. Fan. 2017. *Religion and charity: The social life of goodness in Chinese societies*. Cambridge: Cambridge University Press.

Weller, R.P., and K. Wu. 2017. On the boundaries between good and evil: Constructing multiple moralities in China. *Journal of Asian Studies* 76(1): 47–67. https://doi.org/10.1017/S0021911816001182.

Wells, S. 2017. ***Incarnational ministry: Being with the church.*** Grand Rapids, MI: Wm. B. Eerdmans.

Wickeri, P.L. 2007. ***Reconstructing Christianity in China: K. H. Ting and the Chinese church.*** Maryknoll, NY: Orbis.

Wielander, G. 2009. Bridging the gap? An investigation of Beijing intellectual house church activities and their implications for China's democratization. ***Journal of Contemporary China*** 18: 849–864.

Wielander, G. 2011. Beyond repression and resistance: Christian love and China's harmonious society. ***China Journal*** 65: 119–139. https://doi.org/10.1086/tcj.65.25790560.

Wielander, G. 2013. ***Christian values in communist China.*** London: Routledge.

Wilfred, F. 2014a. Asian Christianity and public life: The interplay. In ***The Oxford handbook of Christianity in Asia***, ed. F. Wilfred. Oxford: Oxford University Press. https://doi.org/10.1093/oxfordhb/9780199329069.013.0035.

Wilfred, F. 2014b. Christian social engagement in Asia. In ***Oxford handbook of Christianity in Asia***, ed. F. Wilfred, 328–342. Oxford: Oxford University Press.

Wilson, B.R. 1966. ***Religion in secular society.*** Harmondsworth: Penguin.

Winter, B. 1994. ***Seek the welfare of the city: Christians as benefactors and citizens. First-century Christians in the Graeco-Roman world.*** Grand Rapids, MI: Eerdmans.

Woodhead, L. 2013. New forms of public religion: Spirituality in global civil society. In ***Religion beyond its private role in modern society***, eds. W. Hofstee, and A. van der Kooij, 29–52. Leiden: Brill.

Wright, T., and T. Zimmerman-Liu. 2013. Atheist political activists turned Protestants: Religious conversion among Chinese dissidents. ***Journal of Church and State*** 57: 268–288.

Wu, F., and K.M. Chan. 2013. Graduated control and beyond: The evolving Government-NGO relations. ***China Perspectives*** 3(91): 9–17.

Wu, K. 2016. The philanthropic turn to religions in post-Mao China: Bureaucratization, professionalization, and the making of a moral subject. ***Modern China*** 43(4): 1–31. https://doi.org/10.1177/0097700416675310.

Yan, Y. 2014. The moral implications of immorality: The Chinese case for a new anthropology of morality. ***Journal of Religious Ethics*** 42(3): 460–493.

Yang, C.K. 1961. ***Religion in Chinese societies: A study of contemporary social functions of religion and some of their historical factors.*** Berkeley: University of California Press.

Yang, F. 2005. Lost in the market, saved at McDonald's: Conversion to Christianity in urban China. ***The Journal for the Scientific Study of Religion*** 44(4): 423–442.

Yang, F. 2006. The red, black, and gray markets of religion in China. ***The Sociological Quarterly*** 47: 93–122.

Yang, G. 2009. ***The power of the internet in China: Citizen activism online.*** New York: Columbia University Press.

Yang, G. 2015. ***China's contested internet.*** Denmark: Nordic Institute of Asian Studies Press.

Yang, H. 2010. The contextualization of Chinese Christian theology and its main concerns. In ***Christianity and Chinese culture***, eds. M. Ruokanen, and P. Huang, 197–204. Grand Rapids, MI: W.B. Eerdmans.

Yao, K.X. 2011. Chinese evangelicals and social concerns: A historical and comparative perspective. In ***After imperialism: Christian identity in China and the global evangelical movement***, eds. R.R. Cook, and D.W. Pao, 46–72. Eugene, OR: Pickwick Publications.

Ye, X. 2006. Message of peace and harmony from the East to the West. In ***Pilgrims and citizens: Christian social engagement in East Asia today***, ed. M.N.-C. Poon, 17–22. Adelaide: ATF Press.

Young, L., and C. Harrison, eds. 2004. *Systemic functional linguistics and critical discourse analysis: Studies in social change.* New York: Continuum.

Yuan, Y. 2018. China's WeChat hits 1bn user accounts worldwide. *Financial Times.* 5 March. https://www.ft.com/content/8940f2d0-2059-11e8-a895-1ba1f72c2c11 (accessed 20 May 2018).

Zhang, J., and Z. Ji. 2018. Lay Buddhism in contemporary China: Social engagements and political regulations. *The China Review* 18(4): 11–39.

Zhang, L. 2017. Woguo shequ fazhan jincheng zhong de yizuo xin lichengbei. Ministry of Civil Affairs. http://www.mca.gov.cn/article/yw/jczqhsqjs/cxsyq/201710/20171000006238.shtml (accessed 3 November 2017).

Zhang, S. 2008. Cong jinde gongyi zhanwang you xinyang Beijing de gongyi shiye fazhan. In *Zhongguo zongjiao gongyi shiye de huigu yu zhanwang*, eds. S. Zhang, and D. Wei, 1–24. Beijing: Zongjiao wenhua chubanshe.

Zheng, Y. 2008. *Technological empowerment: The internet, state, and society in China.* Stanford, CA: Stanford University Press.

Zhuo, X. 2000. Religion and morality in contemporary China. *Irish Theological Quarterly* 65(1): 65–71.

Zuo, F. 2015. *Jidu zongjiao yu jinxiandai zhongguo shehui gongzuo.* Beijing: Minzhu chubanshe.

Index